Is your German not the yellow from the egg? Is your English all under the pig? Well, my friend, you need Denglisch for Better Knowers! Here, two English authors lead a hilarious expedition through some of the German language's greatest expressions, proverbs and possibilities, and wrap them up for international delivery in the form of Denglisch. This book is not only great fun, but also the perfect way to introduce the humble Ausländer (or remind forgetful German readers) of the absolute awesomeness of the German language! While it has been previonaly so maligned and misunderstood, now everyone will discover: with the German language is very good cherry eating!

Liability waiver

All anecdotes in this book use the personal pronoun ›I‹, blending them into a lumpy past-tense soup. Sorry about that. It's just easier than refering to us individually each time. We're as confused as you are, about who we are. Similarly, whenever we end a joke with a punch line involving »my German girlfriend« – it is also not the same woman, which would be weird. It is, in fact, two separate, wonderful German girlfriends, who were combined into a single character and plot device, giving both of us authors plausible deniability for everything questionable that we've written about them.

Authors

Adam Fletcher is a 31 year old bald Englishman. After several years in this fine nation, he'd consider himself almost German, were it not for continued inability to separate his *Akkusativ* from his *Dativ* and his plastic recycling from his paper. When not writing books and articles about his adopted nation, he mostly spends his days eating chocolate, and napping. In fact, no matter what time of day you're reading this, there is a 87.4 % chance that he is napping. *Shhhh!* He is also the author of the *Spiegel* bestselling book, *How to be German*.

Paul Hawkins is a writer, liar, and astronaut, whose life-long pilgrimage to avoid a ›proper‹ job has recently bought him to the Mecca of Delayed Responsibility that is Berlin. In between murdering the German language and apologising for himself, he is still shamelessly insisting on writing comedy books, articles and scripts.

Adam Fletcher
Paul Hawkins

Denglisch for Better Knowers

*Fun Birds, Smart Shitters, Hand Shoes and
more craziness with the amazing German language*

Ullstein

Visit us online:
www.ullstein-taschenbuch.de

Original edition at Ullstein Taschenbuch
1st edition May 2014
© Ullstein Buchverlage GmbH, Berlin 2014
Cover illustration and cover design: Robert M. Schöne
Illustrations inside the book: Robert M. Schöne
Typesetting: KompetenzCenter, Mönchengladbach
Typeset in Officina Sans/Berkeley
Paper: Pamo Super von Arctic Paper Mochenwangen GmbH
Print and binding: CPI books GmbH, Leck
Printed in Germany
ISBN 978-3-548-37536-6

A note from the Authors

Dearest Reader,

If you're anything like us, you may have met people who while not knowing much about the German language, have the following prejudices about it:

1. »German is so harsh! *SCHMETTERLING!* Ha! Even the word for ›butterfly‹ sounds like two angry robots wrestling to their deaths!«
2. »Look how long its words are! *Streichholzschachtel!* That's hilarious!«
3. »Did you hear what Mark Twain said about The Awful German Language? He basically said it was invented by a lunatic with an affinity for never ending nouns and should be quietly retired as a world language …«
4. »*Schadenfreude* is a pretty good word. English doesn't have a word for *Schadenfreude*. German Language: 1, English Language: 2487.«

If you're anything like us, you also know that's a load of nonsense. Most languages sound harsh to a foreign ear, or when just shouted angrily, which people making fun of German tend to do. There are reasons why the words are longer, which, once explained, reveal an awesome kind of language genius. Mark Twain is funny, but misses all the joys of the language's apparent complexity. As for *Schadenfreude*, it is just the most popular gleaming prize on a huge shelf of German's lesser known trophies.

In short, we believe that the German language is badly in need of a re-brand to challenge these out-dated stereotypes. It's about time that someone did something nice for it, and we want to be that someone(s). The fact that it's not our native language is no disadvantage, since it makes it easier for us to find joy and awe in the simple things like an idiom the average German has said a thousand times, without ever thinking about the individual words that comprise it.

This book is a love letter to the German language. We hope you enjoy it.

Liebe Grüße,
Adam and Paul.

P.S. We know Denglisch is a made up word with several different definitions depending on who uses it. Here it's taking an existing German word, phrase or idea (even if its true origin might be an even older culture or language), and translating it into English.

Introduction

There was a time when English and German were like an inseparable young couple that acted, dressed and sounded alike. Indeed, it was difficult to tell where one ended and the other began.

Then, as time and bitterness aged them, ravaging their relationship, cracks in their union began to show. First, they began to sleep in separate beds, then separate rooms, then separate houses, then eventually were estranged to separate landmasses, forever to be divided by water, war and France, in denial of all the good times they once shared.

German turned in upon itself, to lick its wounds in isolation, broken only by the occasional visit from an affable Swiss or Austrian. English, meanwhile, went on the opposite journey. Making up for lost time, it gleefully discarded its inhibitions, flirted with exotic influences, and compromised the world over in an attempt to entertain the masses. It forgot its roots, abandoned its genders, and sucked in foreign vocabulary from all corners of the globe. Some might even say that the language of Shakespeare cheapened itself in its frivolous rush to please and popularise. In other words, it slept around.

Meanwhile, prickly and unforgiving, German trundled slowly forward, like a slow but sturdy horse-and-cart, being increasingly honked at by impatient English cars coming up behind it. It wouldn't be long, indeed, before German's sweet, former lover had been cemented in place as the lingua franca, destined always to be the loudest voice in newly global conversations.

Today, German seems to be increasingly under attack from all sides, whether it be outsiders abandoning its study in their schools, in favour of trendier languages like Spanish, Esperanto, and Mandarin, or from within, from its youth, and the marketing departments of its companies, ever quicker to reach for the shiny, new Anglicism – having their thoughts *upgedatet, upgeloadet, gepostet* and *outgesourcet* into English, while perfectly good and equivalent German words are left shunned like beautiful, antique furniture that's swapped for trendy, flat-pack crap.

While the kind of people who own tambourines might argue that it doesn't matter which language we're all using just as long as we understand each other, we must also protect what is being lost. Wielded in the right, crafted hands, German is unparalleled in its ability to precisely articulate its speaker's thoughts. More importantly, like all languages, German is much, much more than just a collection of words. It's the toolkit which you can use to unpick and understand the mind and ideas of an entire culture – the one that once bore the title of Poets and Thinkers.

Germans are understandably attached with great reverence to their beautiful words, expressions and idioms – even having limited success in infiltrating other languages with some of them, such as *Kindergarten*, *Rucksack*, *Gesundheit* or *Zeitgeist* – but sadly, these words tend to sit alone in an occasional English sentence, lonely and afraid like lost children in a forest. The full, awe-worthy power of German remains largely impenetrable to all but the most patient and forgiving *Ausländer* who is willing to put in the hundreds of hours of study. Many learners find that the German grammar trips them up so often and so cruelly that at some point, they just stay down, play dead, and retreat back to the soft, cuddly safety of English, embarrassed to utter much more than »*zwei Bier, bitte*« in their local *Kneipe*.

As English grows in its global and cultural influence, it seems the amount Germans will be forced to speak it will only increase. There is another option, however, which we call Denglisch. While it may initially appear as if we are just taking the clumsiest nouns and idioms of the German language and translating them literally into English for fun, it is much more than that. Denglisch is a chance to take the beautiful phrasings and ideas of the German people, and present them to the *Ausländer*, gift wrapped in the familiar words of his language, so that they may understand them. It is a chance to teach. It is a chance to give back.

With their defences lowered, the *Ausländer* will be left naked and exposed to the full primal power contained within the mind and imagination of German culture. They will learn. They will be impressed. They will respect and appreciate the beauty that the German language can offer. Even when they hear those Denglisch terms which don't translate all that well or even seem a bit silly in English, we will point out why there is still a valid reason for the *Ausländer* to adopt them into their kiddy toy language.

What follows is a personal collection of our favourite expressions, idioms, compound words and other linguistic possibilities offered by the German language, divided into the different areas of life where they are most likely to be relevant.

Now, you may be met with resistance. Some confusion. Perhaps even complete bafflement. But persist! The *Ausländer* may be initially unwilling to accept exactly why they shouldn't *ask after sunshine, eat cherries with you, or reach you the water*. However, even if Denglisch is not immediately *the yellow of their eggs*, or if they protest to *understand only train station*, you must be insistent that *you mean nothing for ungood*. Don't worry, this book will help on your noble quest.

Denglisch in the Office

Das Konzept ist zu fuzzy.
Wir müssen durch den clutter breaken!

In 2006, the Governor of Baden-Württemberg, Günther Oettinger, declared that English will be the language of work, German will be that of family and free time, the language in which one reads at home (»*Englisch wird die Arbeitssprache, Deutsch bleibt die Sprache der Familie und der Freizeit, die Sprache, in der man Privates liest.*«)

His sentiments caused a small amount of controversy. While some people enjoyed the idea of speaking German only in the safety of their own homes, like a naughty little secret, many did not. By many, of course, we mean most of the country's eighty-two million people. So many so, in fact, that good old Günther was awarded the honourable title of »Language Abuser of the Year« (»*Sprachpanscher des Jahres*«) for his absurd statement.

While Mr Oettinger may have waved his little white flag at the first sign of a word being *outgesourcet* to the English language, he may have had some small point. If there is one area that Anglicisms have been particularly penetrative, it is in the meeting rooms, PowerPoint presentations and bullshit bingo of the modern German office. As the internet continues to shrink the world like a jumper left too long in the wash, and more international German businesses trade in

English, it's ever more tempting to dip your hands into the cookie jar marked »foreign words«, even if they're only being used by Germans, talking to Germans, in German, in Germany. You may have observed such a curious phenomenon.

Then they take these words back home with them – right back into Günther's final bastion of pure German-speaking hope. One day, we'll be there, with our families, in our leisure time, reading our private things, and then all of a sudden we'll notice someone start talking about how »*Der Computer rebootet nicht. Ich wollte doch mit einem High Society Groupie flirten und chatten. Ich bekomme einfach kein Happy Ending.*« or »*Birthday Parties sind immer ein Highlight. Tolle Happenings mit Happy Hour. Da profitiere ich von all meinen social tools und features. Ich bin ein Ladykiller!*«

So what can you do? Well, you can push back! The English language has proved just how pervasive certain catchy (and meaningless) office phrases can be. You know, *pushing envelopes, reinventing wheels, singing from hymn sheets, getting ducks in a row, thinking outside boxes.* Bullshit bingo phrases like these are now used internationally, creeping into the offices of other countries and other languages, even though just about no one remembers where they came from, who said them first, or even what they mean. Well, if no one really knows the meaning or origins of their current office bullshit anyway, why not package up a few superior German office clichés for international Denglisch delivery?

Through inter-company e-mails, morning scrum meetings, whispered cubicle gossip and idle chit-chat around the water cooler, the office is the classroom in which our international colleagues can be given their daily dose of Denglisch. German language enthusiasts need only scatter the seeds of their language all across the world, and wait for them to bloom.

Hello together *(Hallo zusammen)*

Anyone whose global company is armed with an office of affable, hard-working and fastidious Germans is likely to have received a mass e-mail from them that begins *»Hello together«* – the Denglisch for »Hallo zusammen« – used in the place of the English »Hi all«. In fact, in my first job here there was a woman who shouted it loudly each morning, as she walked past our open-plan office. Why is it superior to »Hi all«? The difference, while subtle, should be obvious. The English »Hi all« is about one greeting many. It separates. It says man is, in fact, an island. Meanwhile, *»Hello together«* is a superior group greeting. It gently reinforces to the foreigner the importance of solidarity. Union. Companionship. That their island is really rather more of a group of islands, an archipelago, if you will, and they shouldn't forget that, at least if they want to avoid an office-based mutiny.

Party Evening *(Feierabend)*

Every culture likes a little partying after it finishes the main business of the day. Whether that means a few pints in the local pub after a day's work in the city, a fireside drum-banging after you've built a new mud-hut, or even an igloo-pop disco after you've stockpiled the year's supply of blubber. There are few cultures, however, that could trust their citizens enough to wish them a nice *Party Evening* at whatever time of day that they finish work, whether it is night, afternoon, or even controversially, morning. It's a concept ripe for misuse; only safe in the most sensible and trusted German hands. Wish a Spanish paperboy »Nice Party Evening« after his morning round, and handfuls of confusing, uninvited fireworks might blast their way into the village's naptime. Wish a boisterous Brazilian binman »Nice Party Evening« before the morning rush-hour, and there will be a thousand car traffic jams, honking uselessly behind a colourful feather-covered parade. Wish the humble Russian baker »Nice Party Evening«, and he would be vodka-sodden and entirely flammable by lunch. Meanwhile, it is only the fastidious and reliable Germans that will be patient and respectful enough to celebrate modestly and quietly until the rest of normal society knocks off to join them in their revelry.

Chair Farter *(Sesselpupser)*

A person whose job consists of little more than pushing a pen around while making one chair less easy to steal.

AN ARROGANT PERSON WHO LOVES WORK SO MUCH
SO THAT THEY REFUSE TO POOP ON THE TIME
AND COST OF THEIR EMPLOYER,
PREFERRING INSTEAD TO INFLICT THE
CONSEQUENCES OF THEIR REPRESSED BOWELS
UPON THEIR SMART-SHITTING COLLEAGUES.

Smart Shitter *(Klugscheißer)*

An arrogant person who hates work so much that they try to poop as much as they can on the time and cost of their employer.

Egg Swinging *(Eierschaukeln)*

The English language is severely lacking in poetic vocabulary to define idlers. It has *layabout*, which is bland, uninspired, and can be forgotten by the end of the sentence. *Layaround*, was it? *Be-about*, maybe? Who knows. The same cannot be said of German, which communicates its meaning perfectly, while also provoking a striking visual image that lingers in the mind of its audience. Like *chair farting*. Poetic and precise. A mental image that burns its meaning into your brain. As if the subject had not been defined enough, German even goes one step further, clarifying which kind of idler the idler is. As we've already established, a sitting down idler is obviously a *Chair Farter*. So clear, it's tangible. Male, female, doesn't matter: you can almost smell the meaning. But what happens when you take the chair away, leaving a male idler in an equally useless standing position, adding roughly as much value to the company as its coat rack? Well, he's an *Egg Swinger*, of course.

Everything in the green range
(Alles im grünen Bereich)

Life is complex and unwieldy. It's not always easy to know exactly what you're feeling, even during the process of actually feeling it. Especially when people enquire as to your feelings using unspecific measurements like, »ok?« »good?« or »in Ordnung?«. This is where the English language could benefit from *everything in the green range*. It allows you to think of your mood and life not as an abstract fuzzy thing, but a concrete gauge. The sort Homer Simpson might neglect to check at a power plant. Now that you have this gauge, your relationship to your feelings can change. You're no longer binary, either happy or sad. You're a whole range in-between, ever in flux. Traffic jam on the way to work? That's another notch towards red then. The beautiful colleague from marketing smiles at you in the elevator? Bam! Just like that you're back to green. You go with them to the canteen for a coffee, which then makes you thirty minutes late for a meeting with your boss. Back around the gauge we go towards orange. Every time some specific things happen, good or bad, you can imagine your level of happiness moving around the gauge, from a tranquil green range to an angry, feet slamming, shirt ripping, head shaking, Incredible Hulk style red.

THE DENGLISH
Mood-O-Meter

IN ORDNUNG   **NICHT IN ORDNUNG!**

Give me a house number
(Nennen Sie mal eine Hausnummer)

In English office clichés, estimates are called *ballpark figures*. Being that none of us have ever actually played baseball, though, we know ballparks about as well as we know pre-17th century Chinese Dynasties. Thus, the phrase »give me a ballpark figure« really says to us »hey, there's no need to be too accurate in your estimate, please just speculate wildly.« In short, give useless imprecise information that will lead people to the right general area, and then promptly abandon them in it. Hopelessly lost to wolves or lions or vultures or whatever else one might find in the great ballpark of office nightmares. A house number, though. Now that's something you can work with. It stands in front of a fixed, immovable building. You can ring its bell. You can ask the neighbours. You can sit outside it in your car, watching its residents through eye holes you've cut into yesterday's newspaper. Bring supplies. Bring biscuits. Wait it out. The information will have to come home eventually, and when it does, you'll be ready.

DENGLISCH VERBOTEN!

Colleagues,

A reminder — we speak a fully developed language which is not lacking in words.

Anyone caught using the following verbal molestations; please put €1 in the Anglicism jar. I've helpfully included the correct German word, in case you've forgotten it:

Downloaden	*Herunterladen*
Outsourcen	*Ausgliedern*
Upgraden	*Aufrüsten*
Forwarden	*Weiterleiten*
Enforcen	*Durchsetzen*
Follow-Uppen	*Nachverfolgen*
Highlighten	*Hervorheben*
Overengineeren	*Verkomplizieren*
Twittern/Facebooken	*Zeit verbraten*
Brainstormen	*Zeit verbraten*

Thanks,
THE MANAGEMENT

ANGLIZISMUS-GLAS
BITTE NICHT INSTAGRAMMEN

My Dear Mister Singing Club's School of Denglisch: Umlaut envy

In these School of Denglisch essays, we discuss a particular part of the German language that thrills us, and discuss in a little more length why it should thrill you too.

As previously discussed, English is the slutty village bicycle of languages. Everyone's had a ride, parked it, then applied the *bicycle erection*. While it is often suggested that because of its greedy range of influences, English has a more diverse and expansive vocabulary than any other language, it also means it has a more diverse and expansive range of those languages' collective nonsense.

Take spelling, for example. While other languages with the Roman alphabet used umlauts and accents to bend the 26 little symbols to their correct pronunciation, standardising into a consistent phonetic system, English looked at its French, Latin, Germanic and Scandinavian hodgepodge of mismatched sounds and spellings, and merely surrendered to the madness.

If languages were people, English would be an irrational lunatic, arbitrarily teasing and torturing its poor dyslexics, naked, on a roof, and screaming at the wind, »YOU SPELLED ›PHOENIX‹ WRONG, IDIOT!!«

By comparison, German is a speller's dream. An almost perfectly consistent system of letters and matching sounds.

Like a caring bystander at the bottom of the building, it looks up at the naked English maniac, and gently suggests, ›Phönix?‹

If this all sounds rather hyperbolic, and you can't imagine that the English language could ever suffer umlaut envy, then you're sadly mistaken. We're not above waiting until you're all not looking and stealthily pilfering from your umlaut aisle, using our ill-gotten gains with a casual disregard for accuracy and applicability. Take the now defunct English kitchen company Möben. They fought the Advertising Standards Agency for some five years for the right to use their umlaut, after a complaint was made by a customer that it wrongly implied they were German, when actually they were based on a trading estate in Manchester.

Möben's reasoning? Everyone knows German engineering is good (those long in memory may note a certain irony here, since originally in the 19th century the British added »Made in Germany« to German products to warn of their low quality). From those Huf Haus modular kits to the little wooden toys Germans staunchly believe are educationally superior. Möben wanted people to take them seriously. To achieve this, they needed an umlaut. So, Moben became Möben. It would be like if we, to support our careers as observers of German culture, changed our names to Päul Häwkins and Ädäm Fletscher.

It's not just in the world of furniture, there's also something known as ›the metal umlaut‹. Mötley Crüe are probably the most famous example of it, with Motörhead a close second. I like to imagine their renegade umlauting comes back to haunt them when on tour here in Germany, and everyone keeps introducing them as »Moetley Cruee«. It's Motley, guys. M-O-T-L-E-Y. »The umlauts are just for show, it's not a real umlaut«, they'd plead. The audience would stare back, mouths aghast. »What do you mean, *it's not a real umlaut? It's just for show*? Umlauts are serious business, heavily-tattooed foreigner! They're not like a funny novelty moustache you can just stick to the upper lip of your O.«

Clearly, what is needed in the English language is some small revolution of good sense, to stop generation after generation perpetuating the dogmatic nonsense spelling of their parents. How many more generations will put their ›phoenix‹ layer upon ›phoenix‹ layer, until someone brave enough eventually pulls the whole structure down, and builds a new one in its place labelled *Phönix*?

English won't change itself. Evolution doesn't mean that everything gets better and better and better. It just means stubborn things survive. Indeed, an evolved thing is merely the sum of the maximum possible number of mistakes that could be made while still perpetuating it. Humans have stupid little toes and an appendix that sometimes explodes for no reason. English has its spelling.

English must be changed, then. We must look to better, foreign examples like German to learn from. Take, for example, the perfectly ordinary English sentence: *the bear's heir with the rare hair can make a prayer, eh*?

Gibberish. The vowels in each word are pronounced in the exact same way, but the spellings vary absurdly. It's a sentence that is cruelly booby trapped to trip up children, foreign language learners, and anyone else who is nonconformist and sensible (also known as dyslexics.)

However, with some minor tweaks and the addition of a simple little umlaut, we could harmonise the spelling of all the words and everyone would know how to pronounce them. The sentence from above would become *the bär's här with the rär här can make a prär, ä?*

See, now that makes perfect sense. Since the next generation won't read anything written on dead trees anyway, because it will all be digital, now would be a perfect time to start fixing the English language. ›Books‹ will soon just be distant memories. As I write this, there is a whole bunch of hoo-ha around the revelations of the American PRISM program and general governmental spying. I can't help but think, since they're in there anyway, reading all the words we're writing, they could do a little good. That, like a particularly pernickety teacher, they could get their global red pens out and fix it all up a bit. Maybe crawl the entire backlog of humanity's digitised history with some top secret CIA software, and do one big global »find and replace«, ushering in a new golden era of umlaut led, German inspired, English phoneticism.

Denglisch at Home

A Denglischman's home is his Before Hanging Castle

Your *Party Evening* has finally begun. It's time to pack up your things, put them into your *Backsack*, and head to the warm, practical comfort of your *two-room-Wohnung* for more Denglisch-spreading opportunities.

But wait, isn't that the same *Wohnung* that Günther Oettinger said is the last safe, cherished haven for pure uncensored German-speaking? Isn't that the same *Wohnung* that is already being infiltrated and bombarded with the »cool« new English words and slogans of international products, magazines, newspapers and TV shows?

Once you're locked in your home and away from the world, surely the modest German homestead is the place with the least opportunities to spread the gift of Denglisch?

Not true, comrade. Since most young Germans will make an exchange trip to an English-speaking country at some point in their schooling, we should prepare them for their act of international relations with Denglisch phrases that they can carry across linguistic borders to all corners of the globe.

Then, once they are safely inside the homes of their unsuspecting host families, our Denglisch-equipped young folk, like an army of Trojan horses, can sneak out in the dead of night and lower the defences ready for the Denglisch revolution.

No home shall be safe.

Before Hanging Castle *(Vorhängeschloss)*

What happened to the tough padlocks of old? Once so strong you could trust them to strap down your family during a violent *Wind Trousering*? You know, back when a padlock was not ashamed to be a padlock? Now it seems padlocks can be small, pink, feeble; included in Christmas crackers as novelty gifts, used on tiny suitcase zips, and used by young tourist couples as bridge jewellery, writing their initials on them in little love hearts, and attaching them as permanent reminders of their temporary gooeyness. Yuck. Maybe English needs a new word for the classic, sturdy, secure, dangling fortress kind of padlock. Luckily, Denglisch is ready to protect us: enter the *Before Hanging Castle*. Raising a drawbridge to any onrushing invader, the *Before Hanging Castle* swings defiant!

I hedgehog myself *(Ich igel mich ein)*

Getting up in the morning is one of the worst and most difficult things a human has to do. There you suddenly are, awake, confused, aware, again, and staring at that same old absurd universe as yesterday, still bafflingly beyond your comprehension. The only consolation is that you are laying down, peaceful, warm, and comfortable. But then you remember that something, somewhere, needs doing. *Eugh.* Soon, against all inner protests, you find that you are suddenly and mysteriously up. No one knows how this happens. However, there are some days that you just can't. When you wake up mid-dream, mid-cycle, mid-something – it doesn't matter what you were in the middle of, quite frankly, all you know is that you look and feel like a beaten up flu-victim, and that today is simply not going to happen. It's impossible. It may only be 9am, but it's a write-off. Call work, tell them you're sick, get your laptop and biscuits within range of the duvet, there's only one thing to do and the German language describes it perfectly, *hedgehog yourself.*

You look stupid out of the laundry
(Du guckst dumm aus der Wäsche)

With only a little creativity, there is potential to look stupid in almost any situation. »I think, therefore I am«, would perhaps be more accurate as, »I *Fettnapf,* therefore I am«. For example, while nipping to the corner shop, I once accidentally locked myself in my own porch for five hours – hours that involved having to pee in an old bottle, developing claustrophobia, and renaming a discarded football I'd found, Wilson 2. The only solace I take from sharing this story with you is in knowing that you have your own version of it. Take even the tiniest, littlest, simplest task – in my case, leaving my house – and I guarantee that there is somebody, somewhere, doing it so completely wrong that other people nearby are embarrassed to be mammals. However, very few situations have the potential to go wrong on quite the same magnitude as the laundry, which is probably why the German language reserves it special attention. You can ruin the colour of your clothes, shrink them, forget them, mix them up with someone else's, wash your money, wash your phone, break the machine, break yourself, or any combination of the above which might leave you staggering out of your house or the laundrette, *looking stupid out of the laundry.*

You Lazy Sock *(Du faule Socke)*

Lazy people get a bad rep. In this fast-paced world of global competition, capitalism and consumption, there's little respect for the person who just wants to sit quietly, be still, and contemplate their wondrous existence. Or play video games in their pants. There is something in the German expression *Lazy Sock* however, that respects and redeems the charm of this lifestyle. Sure, you may be a *Lazy Sock*, lying around on the bedroom floor, not adding a huge amount of value to anything, but that doesn't mean you'll one day have to change everything you are just to fit in with society. You know why? Because socks come in pairs (at least they should, see *You look stupid out of the laundry*). Which means there's at least one other special person out there, just like you – getting up too late, taking accidental naps, reheating leftover breakfasts for lunch and dinner. There's hope for you yet, my *Lazy Sock* friend. Unfortunately, it's a statistically unlikely hope because you're both so lazy and housebound you'll probably never meet each other, but it's hope nonetheless.

Warm Showerer *(Warmduscher)*

At first, it may seem a little strange to call someone cowardly a *Warm Showerer,* an insult I've often heard here. The majority of people all over the world seem to prefer warm showers, which means you're sort of calling yourself, everyone you know, and billions of other people, a bunch of wimps. Humanity generally thinks of itself as quite brave, climbing mountains, crossing seas, and heading into outer space, but then you bring them right back down to earth, questioning if they're really tough enough for a little bit of sudden, chilly wetness? Cold showers are good for you, and good for the planet, so what better time to introduce the new Denglisch concept of the *Warm Showerer*? There are lots of forces in the world that want to keep us afraid, and lots of times we come up short when compared to brave characters in movies or adverts. But, there's that one constantly available test of heroism – the German bathroom bravery-testing machine, that's just one twist of the tap away, becoming a cold showerer.

To not have all cups in the cupboard
(Nicht alle Tassen im Schrank haben)

German logic dictates that cups belong in ordentlich cupboards. People who are considered insane, therefore, are discussed as *not having all cups in the cupboard*. While a very nice
expression that could be easily used in other languages as it
is in German, I feel that first it requires further discussion.
Discussion as to why cups would want to be in cupboards.
Why it's right for us to force them in there. Sure, in the cupboard is safety and likely a sense of cup community. One is

with one's cup peers. But, one is also closed off to the wider world, and must live in the dark. I think it's more plausible-that cups want to be out of their cupboards, that they want to be a part of wild kitchen parties, be doused in *Sekt*, have spoons swirled around their innards, to be taken out into beautiful nature for picnics. So really, I ask you, who is truly the insane one? The one who gives in to life's whim and fancy. Or, the one whose organised and regimented life has a fixed place for everything? Who lives to put everything in its rightful cubbyhole. I think it is easily plausible that while the German language is looking at life's eccentrics and remarking on their wayward cups, those same eccentrics are looking right back at us and doing the opposite: »Wow, look at that normal person. Wound a little tight, aren't they? They've definitely got *their cups firmly in their cupboard*.«

Everything for the cat *(Alles für die Katz)*

This old, commonly used idiom correctly recognises that cats are the ones, in fact, that keep humans as pets. The story goes that there was once a kindly blacksmith who did good work, then would let his customers name their price. Sensing an opportunity, those crafty customers then mostly just chose to pay him in ›thank yous.‹ Cheeky *Smart Shitters*. At this point the blacksmith bought a cat, and sat it right at the front of the shop, where all the customers could see it. The next time someone paid him in thanks, the blacksmith replied: »Great, that's for the cat.« At which point he probably made a theatrical gesture towards the hungry animal. Slowly but surely, the cat kept getting paid in words, not money for food. Eventually it died of starvation, which made a powerful point to the customers about just how little nutritional value is contained in gratitude. Assuming they were those same customers. Otherwise it was just a waste of a perfectly good cat.

Half the rent *(Halbe Miete)*

Only after my girlfriend and I had moved in together and had to clean, did she tell me that she »doesn't do bathrooms«. Doesn't »do« them, she said, as if that was all the evidence and reasoning required. There was no discussion about this. It was just presented as a fact, followed by the words *»Ende der Diskussion«*, which is what she tends to say when she's ending discussions. As a result, I clean our bathroom. Rarely, of course, and with a practiced, obvious reluctance. But I do it. In I go, pushing water around with my hands for a few minutes, making funny faces in the mirror, until, as far as I'm concerned, it's »*already half the rent*«. Out I come. Satisfied. In she goes. Dissatisfied. Out she comes. »Your cleaning is only half the rent,« she says. »Great!« I reply. »What do you mean, ›great‹?« she says. »That means I'm done then, right? I only pay half the rent.« – »No,« she says, »you've misunderstood, the expression is either *only half the rent* (nur die halbe Miete) or *already half the rent* (schon die halbe Miete). *Only half the rent* means you'll go back into the bathroom and do it properly if you know what's good for you.« This is when I say: »Sorry … I don't doooo fractions.« Then I run away and hide in the wardrobe. *Ende der Diskussion.*

My Dear Mister Singing Club's School of Denglisch: Compounding is not Frankensteining

Not only is *Schadenfreude* probably the German language's most famous compound creation, it's also the emotion most aptly felt when Germans learn that you can't compound in most other languages. Compounding is much more than just frankensteining words together; a compound word becomes something in its own right, worth more than the sum of its parts, it's a simple case of 2 + 2 = 5.

The joy of compounding is in the stacking of ideas and notions, as if they were language lego bricks. Your oversized hybrid creation can then sit defiantly in the middle of the sentence, blocking access to the verb, like a padlocked fire exit. It also offers the rare linguistic pleasure of bunching up three of the same letter in a row – did I tell you about my ancestress (*Stammmutter*)? She was not only bullet-proof (*schusssicher*), but also a conductor for the Zoo Orchestra (*Zooorchester*).

Back to *Schadenfreude*. The Oxford English Dictionary incorporated the word all the way back in 1982 defined as »malicious enjoyment at the misfortunes of others«. It takes English six full words and 35 characters more just to summarize the precision offered by the compound *Schadenfreude*.

Since the English language can't compound, our solution

is simply to throw more words at the problem and hope something sticks. Take for example, the word *Schreibtischtäter*. *Schreib* (write) + *Tisch* (table) + *Täter* (criminal) = Desk Criminal. An idea like that is hard to convey in English. White Collar Criminal? Desk Dictator? To get around the problem, we mostly just call them *Politicians*.

Here are some of my favourite compounds, and their Denglisch equivalents:

Backpfeifengesicht: slapface (someone whose face begs to be slapped)

Leistungsfähigkeitsverstärkung: achievementcapacity-strengthening (productivity improvement)

Vergangenheitsbewältigung: historicalconciliation (the act of coming to terms with the past)

Schattenparker: shadeparker (a person who only parks in the shade, someone who's a bit of a wimp)

Zusammengehörigkeitsgefühl: togetherbelongingsfeeling (feelings of solidarity)

Lebensabschnittsgefährte: lifephasepartner (someone who while very welcome in your bed today, might not be invited back there tomorrow)

Brustwarzenvorhof: breastwartfrontcourtyard (areola)

Sure, English gets there, it can find equivalents, but it has to take the scenic route. More words allow for more misinterpretations. There's a famous quote attributed in turns to Pascal, Voltaire, Mark Twain, Karl Marx and Goethe: »I have made this letter longer than usual, only because I have not had the time to make it shorter.« At a push, the German language could probably have reduced that entire letter into one monstrous, 4-page word featuring character development and plot twists.

Of course, the *Smart Shitters* among you might reply, but you can compound in English! Stop day|dreaming every|body! Don't for|get, many English words have such a partner|ship, master|pieces you use every|day, but the back|grounds of which we for|get.

Those are good for a start, but we're limited to convention and a loyalty to our dictionary overlords, like children told only to colour within the lines. We're not allowed to just go around making it up. Well, we can, of course, but no one will congratulate us for our cleverness and poetry. They will just back away from us slowly, leaving us to suffer with our *repressedcompoundenvy* from our inability to *complex-visual-sentencewordplayconstruct*.

Denglisch with Others

Meaning nothing for ungood with lovers, friends and family

International relationships are a little bit like solving a jigsaw puzzle without having the box. While a great source of humourous, linguistic and cultural friction, you do spend a lot of time grappling around trying things, looking for those little corner pieces of shared understanding. Not good? Turn it around. Try it now. Better? Nope, still doesn't fit. My bad. *Nothing for ungood.* With every joke that falls flat, every idiom that needs explaining, every 90s indie band or c-list actor that must be googled, your partner stares back from outside the comfortable warmth of context.

»Wait, wait, wait! What do you mean you've not seen ›Charlie and the Chocolate Factory‹? Stop everything right now. I can't continue in a relationship for even a second longer with someone who doesn't know what an Oompa Loompa is. »Oompa Loompa do-ba-dee-dee, if you are wise you'll listen to me … I want it *downgeloadet* this very instant!«

The joy is in how that friction allows you both to hold up a mirror to each other's cultures. Where something as simple as misunderstanding one word can derail a whole conversation leading to a tumultuous argument that results in two grown adults wrestling each other in the Supermarket's yoghurt aisle.

»*So ein Mist!*«

»What have you missed? The bus doesn't leave for ages yet.«

»No, *Mist*!«

»But it's sunny. There's no mist. Are you seeing things again? I keep telling you, you need glasses.«

»Shut up! *Mensch. Wirklich! Du gehst mir so auf den Keks.*«

»Cookies? What's with cookies? Probably a bit ›misty‹ for cookies.«

»I'm going to hit you now and I consider that perfectly justified.«

Or where a simple idiom you've said a thousand times yet never once thought about the meaning and origin of, can be re-evaluated under the icy stare and careful questioning of an *Ausländer.*

»Yeah, well, relax, *nothing will be eaten as hot as it's cooked.*«

»You're going to cook? I am getting a bit peckish.«

»No, idiot. You've not heard that expression? Didn't they teach you anything in that funky foreign school of yours? Maybe if you studied a little longer, you wouldn't be so clueless, Mr Three Year Bachelor in Media Nonsense.«

Denglisch can help. It can be the language equivalent of inter-cultural bridge building, wrapping the foreign in the familiar.

Birding *(Vögeln)*

It's believed by some that humans first discovered kissing from observing birds feeding their young. The observation didn't end there though, as far as the German language was concerned. While the prudish of other nations looked away, they continued spying on our feathered friends in the supposed privacy of their nests to see what else they were getting up to. This is probably how they came up with the term *vögeln*, or in Denglisch, *birding*. One has to wonder about the person who first linked the act of human love-making to that of *birding*, and what exactly it was that they were doing in the bedroom that caused them to see this similarity in the first place. Actually, if you want to go that far, you might go one step further still and think about the poor person that was on the receiving end of all that eager, deranged, energetic flapping. Generally, if you are making love, and your arms are banging into bed-side lamps, taking down curtain rods, and causing feathers to go flying everywhere (from the pillows, of course), then consider that you might be doing it too enthusiastically for the enjoyment of other humans, and repeated performances may lead your birding partner to search out the safety of another love nest.

Strange Walk and Side Jump
(Fremdgehen und Seitensprung)

Once we invented cars, airplanes and the internet, the idea of ›The One‹ started to seem slightly outdated. We could suddenly contact, meet and even potentially marry millions of different people! We didn't just have to resign ourselves to marrying our least annoying neighbour, or most handsome colleague. Or even marrying at all. Now we can just find any ›one‹ that we like enough, and then share a timeline with them for as long as we don't want to run away and open a beach bar in Costa Rica. Of course, this is mostly frowned upon by the written laws of marriage. However, it is not frowned upon by the unwritten laws of physics, which makes it entirely possible. As a result, we need new vocabulary for those of us who do more than wonder about the suitability of our current partners, relationships and timelines, and those of us who are brave enough to step out of what we know and either *side jump* (temporarily) or *strange walk* (permanently) into something better.

Emergency horny *(Notgeil)*

The desire to procreate is not like other basic desires, the need for food, shelter or water. It doesn't arrive at regular, spaced intervals like that of breakfast, night time and thirst. The desire to procreate is rather whimsical and urgent, rushing in quickly like a violent storm in reaction to either visual stimulus or just plain old opportunity, creating an inconvenient problem that often needs to be dealt with *now*.

RIGHT NOW! The new Denglisch adjective *emergency horny* encompasses this urgency perfectly.

You grin like a honeycakehorse
(Du grinst wie ein Honigkuchenpferd)

If I were to ask you what your six favourite things in the entire world are, I'm reasonably confident that you will answer – smiling, icing, eating, honey, baked goods, and horses. I'm not the only one. German people are so confident about these six, that they've been busy finding ways to combine and stack them all together, like Jenga, of genius. It was hard going at first, early experiments involving applying icing to actual horses were a failure and if anything represented somewhat of a human-horse relationship low point. But, did the Germans give up? No they did not. They persevered until they created the smiling, iced, edible, honey infused, baked, horse shaped – *honeycakehorse*. The executive summary of all human achievement contained within something small enough to fit in your pocket. So popular did it become that

now anytime someone is displaying overwhelming, sponta-
neous combustion levels of joy and happiness, they are said
to be *grinning like a honeycakehorse.*

You have no idea of tooting and blowing
(Du hast von Tuten und Blasen keine Ahnung)

In the age of the internet, opinions are just a click away. Like
anyone who spends a lot of time online, sampling and collec-
ting up the opinions of others to pass off as my own, I sometimes forget that I'm an idiot. Because, sadly, watching is not
doing. This knowledge is ingrained in every German from
the solid, reliable backbone of their economy: the *Mittelstand.*
Good, solid, family-run businesses, doing things, and doing
those things well. Things are »Made in Germany«, not
»Watched Being Made in Germany«. This new Denglisch
expression should serve to remind the rest of the world that
no matter how many online videos you watch of the world's
greatest saxophonists or tubists, it does not mean *you have
any idea of tooting and blowing.*

I laugh me dead *(Ich lach mich tot)*

Just because laughing is overwhelmingly fun and releases waves of positive hormones, it does not mean Germans can't find a perfectly good reason to be scared of it. In this case, it's that they might actually laugh so much THAT THEY WILL DIE! Let's skirt quickly around the non-existent science supporting such an idea and instead focus on its very German sentiment. Life is serious, and to be treated with respect. Like an expensive vase, it must be handled with care and fear to avoid getting chipped. The foreigner is unlikely to understand this and when they get letters from the German government or GEMA, they'll think their whimsical »I'm on permanent holiday« naivety, or exotic expat charm will get them out of trouble. It won't. If they fail to understand the gravity of the situation, respond to their wise-cracks with a deadly serious »*I laugh me dead*«. Say it slowly. Pause between each word. Look them square in the eye and let them know just how deadly unfunny you're finding them at this particular moment. You might save their life.

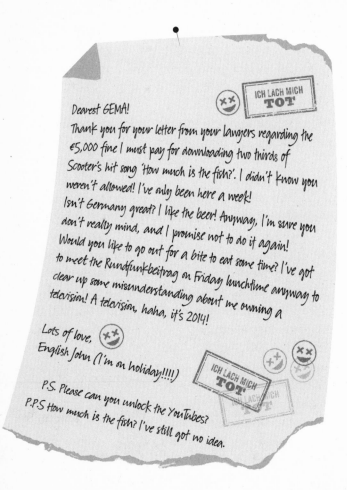

Dearest GEMA!

Thank you for your letter from your lawyers regarding the €5,000 fine I must pay for downloading two thirds of Scooter's hit song 'How much is the fish?'. I didn't know you weren't allowed! I've only been here a week!

Isn't Germany great? I like the beer! Anyway, I'm sure you don't really mind, and I promise not to do it again!

Would you like to go out for a bite to eat some time? I've got to meet the Rundfunkbeitrag on Friday lunchtime anyway to clear up some misunderstanding about me owning a television! A television, haha, it's 2014!

Lots of love,
English John (I'm on holiday!!!!)

P.S. Please can you unlock the YouTubes?
P.P.S How much is the fish? I've still got no idea.

If my grandmother had wheels, she'd be an omnibus (Wenn meine Großmutter Räder hätte, wäre sie ein Omnibus)

In English, if someone makes an unrealistic suggestion, one can respond to them with the affirmation, ›well … yeah … and if my aunty had balls, she'd be my uncle!‹ It's irreverent and funny. Too funny. You're not trying to be whimsical, you're trying to make a point. The point being that they are being too whimsical. You don't argue with a creationist by showing them fossils. You fight irrationality with more irrationality. Fire with fire. Nonsense with nonsense. Your suggestion must be even more ridiculous than theirs, to highlight that the entire conversation you're having is taking place in the Faraway Land of Nonsense. So instead, use the Denglisch expression »*if my grandmother had wheels, she'd be an omnibus*«. Stare at them. Twitch. Remember that the statement is most effective when delivered with both eyes pointing in different directions.

Some of our younger German readers may be a little perplexed that they've not heard of this expression. Surprise! We're all learning here. It's an oldie and has suffered neglect in recent years, but we think it's well worth saving and, thus, encourage you to use it regularly to save it from the big Duden in the sky.

NEXT STOP: PARKBENCH!

Michael

♥ updated his relationship status to "it's complicated"

> **Tolga**
> Equal goes it loose!

> **Annett**
> I don't trust that roastbeef

Michael

♥ is in a relationship with
Scarlett Johansson

24 friends like this

> **Stefanie**
> Overmonkeyhorny! Luckwish!

> **Annett**
> Really? Or are you trying to sell me for stupid?

> **Linn**
> My dear Mr Singing Club! Really well made.

> **Tolga**
> Well, well, well, now you've come in the devil's kitchen.

> **Manuel**
> Very big cinema!

Michael

♥ is now "single"

> **Annett**
> Yeah well, with you was never good cherry eating

> **Linn**
> Nonsense with sauce!

> **Manuel**
> Holla the forestfairy :(

My Dear Mister Singing Club's School of Denglisch: Trennbare Verben and The Great Verb Delay

With the German language, there's never a dull moment. It's like permanently reading a whodunit murder mystery novel; the scene is built, the characters have been introduced, but exactly what happened you don't get to know until that final verb twist at the very end!

This works in two ways, the first is *trennbare Verben*. Very often Germans are unaware what these are called, or even, why they're special. We'd like to do something about that. *Trennbare Verben* are like couples who've suffered messy breakups, then retreated to separate sentence corners to get some space from each other. They belong together, but they live apart. The beauty of the German trennbaren Verb is just how much power you can pack into a tiny little addition to a verb. It's like having a house, and adding on what you think will be a small, brick, one room extension, but then, when it's actually finished, you've really changed the whole composition of the house, tripled the floor space and doubled its market value. Just by adding a few letters to the front of a verb. It's a kind of magic.

So while you quickly reveal *stimmen* to your conversation partner, you can hold back the prefix until the very end. They know your story involves you and a colour-blind elephant, but they don't know if you've voted for it *(abstimmen)*, changed your mind about it *(umstimmen)*, were upset by it *(verstimmen)*, or set something up for it *(anstimmen)* until the final, great prefix reveal.

The second way is that the German language requires you to place a sentence's second verb at the end, which has the same effect as the *trennbare Verb*. You are forced to pay attention until the end of the sentences. You can't switch off, assuming you've already heard all the interesting parts, and what's to come now is just sentence filler in the form of additional description.

Of course that's the rather ›glass is half full‹-perspective. There are often also times in which the sentence I'm saying has rolled on for so long, I've completely forgotten what I was talking about in the first place, and, like a delightfully dotty old man, forget to give the final verb to my German conversation partner. They stare. I wonder why, remember, then blurt out a solitary »sold«, »jumped,« or »ducked.«

But let's assume that's just me, and focus on the positive. Good Germans need good memories.

Denglisch for Fun

Life is a Sugarlicking!

The stereotype of Germans is that they are not the most fun. That's not true. Perhaps the only thing that is true is that they are better at determining the precise time, location and duration of any upcoming fun, well in advance.

I remember when I first moved to Germany, I threw a housewarming party. I was going to be home all day anyway so I didn't specify a time on the invitation, just telling people they could arrive when they wanted. To prove I was open, sociable and whimsical, I think I even wrote ›Whenever o' clock.‹ *Ho ho ho, hilarious Ausländer*, I thought.

It was the wrong joke to the wrong audience.

The get-up-earliers weren't sure if 8pm might appear too over-eager. The go-to-bed-laters whether midnight would make them look too under-eager. It was a social nightmare – what was the correct time to be just eager enough?

Confusion simmered. Worry stirred. Agitation reigned. People laughed at the invitation nervously, then contacted one another before the party, keen not to appear flustered, or uptight in their pursuit of clues as when to everyone else would arrive.

On the night itself, as it got increasingly closer to a normal party-starting time, casual-sounding texts and phone calls starting to come in, as if to say »Haha, good joke, liked that one, ho ho ho … but … seriously … what time?«

»Whenever,« I said.

»Ha ha ha, very good joke again, liked that one, too, ho ho ho … but … seriously … what time?«

»Errr … now?«

»OK. Great. We're outside.«

Let's make party! *(Party machen)*

Hello together,

Last week, I asked you to come to my party at »Whenever o' clock«. I now realise that was not the only mistake on my invitation and in part why the evening did not have the success I, as your humble foreign host, had anticipated. I tried to *have* a party. I tried to *throw* a party. I invited you to come to *my* party. It was because of an inadequacy of my sometimes inferior language. I thought I could just buy some potato salad, play some music, fill the bath with beer, and a party would magically emerge. In German, rightly, you cannot possess a party. You cannot visit it. You cannot create it alone. You must *make* a party. You and me together. Us. Everyone. I realise now your language is right, parties cannot be directed from the top-down by a fun loving, good time dictator, they must be built from the bottom up by the enthusiastic, tireless masses, sharing the responsibility and sharing the rewards. It wasn't called the socialist party for nothing. We all, together, *make a party*.

Mood Canon *(Stimmungskanone)*

There's a footballing expression that says »if the referee is doing a good job, you won't see him«. There's a lot to be said for people who just quietly work away in the background, doing their jobs well, and not seeking plaudits for it. There's one section of humanity that I don't believe have ever heard this expression, nor heeded its wisdom – *Wedding DJs*. This was confirmed to me again recently when I attended my first German wedding in a small town of no obvious redeemable qualities. Firstly, the DJ set up a giant banner with his name and web address across the dance floor. It was more accurately sized to be a Superbowl advert for Pepsi than an oversized local DJ's business card. Despite his job consisting of little more than owning speakers and pressing play on a playlist, he spent the occasion hogging the microphone and attempting to upstage the bride and groom whenever possible by saying completely obvious, redundant things like »doesn't she look wonderful, folks«,

»heeerrreee comes the happy coupppllleee!«, and »the buffet is now open«. Once the evening arrived, everyone was told to be quiet because he had a surprise for us. He then ran around adjusting the room's lights before starting a countdown from ten that culminated in him switching on a whole range of curious spinning, flashing, flipping, multicoloured DJ lights, and balls, and a smoke machine that signified that the empty dance floor was open. As he did this, in a beautiful moment of understated German irony, the guest next to me – who had become increasingly annoyed with the DJ over the course of the evening – shouted a deadpan »*Stim-*

mungskanone« at him and began slowly clapping. Rarely have so few words, expressed so much sarcasm, so perfectly. He was a *Mood Canon*.

Here is dead trousers *(Hier ist tote Hose)*

In most languages, when a party ›has life‹, it is considered good. If it ends with clothes all over the floor, obviously, it is considered even better. Champagne all round! If it doesn't have either of these things, and doesn't look like it is ever going to, then a qualified party doctor should be called. Only once they have checked the pulse and confirmed the time, may they finally declare that any potential for fun is well beyond resuscitation. This is best achieved with the Denglisch pronouncement, ›*Here is dead trousers*.‹ Apparently the origin of the phrase is that of men with erectile dysfunction,

who are said to possess *dead trousers*, which is a slightly curious expression and we feel cruelly misrepresents the real sexual veracity of leg wear.

Fun Bird *(Spaßvogel)*

Fun Birds are the life of any party – the ones arriving late with a bottle of Jagermeister, a Cuban cigar, four strangers they just met in the car park, cracking jokes, the first and the last ones on the dance floor. Like with other bird-watching activities, it's easier to spot some *Fun Birds* more than others. There are big, obvious peacocks and subtle, little bushtits. Some have underwear on the outside of their trousers, ties wrapped around the heads, and wacky, colourful hats, tipped slightly askew – these are the people who have decided themselves that they are fun, and are informing you visually just in case you hadn't noticed. Other *Fun Birds* are much more subtle – hovering in the corners of the room, quietly daring their friends to try and drink an entire pint of beer in under a minute using only a teaspoon. When *Fun Birds* are around, the trousers are not just fully erect, but in danger of coming off at any moment.

Fun Brake *(Spaßbremse)*

Fun Brakes are an underappreciated but equally important part of any good party, in the exact same way that brakes are an incredibly important part of any good car. Sure, you might think it's fun to drive full-blast into the *Party Evening*, but do you know how parties end without *Fun Brakes*? They crash into trees, plummet over cliffs, or shoot into the air from unfinished motorway bridges just like in popular Hollywood films. *Fun Brakes* are actually party-enablers, party-stabilisers, essential fun-lubricants. The silent, serious heroes. *Fun Brakes* are there to help make introductions, buy toilet rolls, top up the ice, and dissuade drunken *Fun Birds* from trying to climb tall trees or high fences. *Fun Brakes* really come into their own towards the end of the night, when cabs need to be called, mess needs to be cleaned up, neighbours need to be calmed, police officers pacified, fires extinguished, and over-eager *Fun Birds* must be peeled from bathroom floors and put to nest.

Head Cinema *(Kopfkino)*

Head Cinema is a beautiful expression that the English language desperately needs so we can better describe the phenomenon of having your thoughts hijacked. Of lying in bed and trying fruitlessly to sleep, but ending up only staring at the ceiling as your imagination loops endless movies you'd never wanted to see. Movies with titles like *»Remember That Time In Gym Class When You Were 12 And Your Trousers Fell Down?«*,

»*You Still Didn't Do Your Tax Return 4*«, or »*Your Wife Is Getting Kind of Friendly With That Guy Alan at Work, Isn't She?*«. Movies that all seem to star you, only not as the movie's plucky young star; the one who overcomes all odds and triumphs in a climactic but ultimately joyous finale that involves a bollywood style mass dance scene and the release of several dozen white doves. No, you're not that character. You're the character who crosses the road whilst texting and gets hit by a bus.

Very big cinema *(Ganz großes Kino)*

You know how it goes. It's Saturday morning. You're hungry. You go out to buy milk, and somehow you get in a car chase. You try to pay for the milk, and cause several deaths and the financial ruin of a large bank. You try to leave the shop, then a casual glance at another customer triggers the sudden, dramatic unfolding of a powerful, timeless love story. It's all very inconvenient and distracting – you only wanted muesli, why does this keep happening to you? Why does life keep burdening you with the problems and over-exaggerations of other, far less rational people? People who, from the smallest tiniest little melodramas somehow manage to create a ›Lord of the Rings‹ style trilogy, casting you in its starring role. The Denglisch expression *Very big cinema* when coupled with a nonchalant ironic tone, reminds people that just because they're capable of making a mountain from a molehill, it doesn't mean they actually should and if they choose to, they shouldn't deposit said mountain between you and your morning muesli.

Hand Shoes *(Handschuhe)*

For most foreigners learning German, I'm sure that finding out gloves are called *Handschuhe* (*Hand Shoes*) is a moment of sweet poetry. It was certainly a personal highlight for me. Indeed, I've worn gloves every day since, just so I can continually refer to them in conversation. *Handschuhe*. *Hand Shoes*. Lovely. It's like someone just took the English language out for a picnic, played it a song on the ukulele, and then offered it cake. It's adorable. Pure language Disneyfication.

Of course, this is the moment in which I'd normally attempt to convince you that the English language is in some way disadvantaged by having the word glove and not *Hand Shoes*. That is not the case. Glove is a fine word, and part of many fine expressions, such as rule with a velvet glove. So, let's put logic aside. When I was seven, I wanted a pony. Did I need a pony? I did not. Was that relevant? It was not. Not all wants are rational. Now I'm a grown adult, and I want my native language to have the word *Hand Shoes*. It would fit English like a *Hand Shoe*. Give me what I want, NOW, or the *Hand Shoes* are really going to come off.

Denglisch Travels

Leaving the Church in the Village

Germans travel fantastically well. In fact, in 2002 the travel company Expedia did a worldwide survey, and voted them as the world's best tourists! Perhaps it's because Germany isn't famous for the hospitality of its own service industry staff that German hearts are so easily conquered by the smiling cultures of faraway lands.

True, German travellers tend to blend in about as successfully as a corporate accountant in the center of a vegan, reggae drum circle. But that can also be a good thing; something that only helps to accentuate their good qualities. They'll speak your language better than you can, and are not above correcting your grammar just to demonstrate that fact. They'll turn up fifteen minutes before they said they'd arrive, standing at the exact specific point of where you were supposed to meet. If you agree to meet at a restaurant, they tend to wait outside for you, like a kind host waiting to greet you and saving you the hassle of having to go in to try and find them.

They'll have researched the nuances of your culture whilst planning their *Project Holiday* and they'll know all the things they can and can't say. They won't make inappropriate jokes.

Unless, of course, yours is a culture that reveres inappropriate jokes above all others, in which case they will have pre-planned the most awful things to call your mother weeks in advance as a charming sign of cultural diplomacy.

You're on the woodway *(Du bist auf dem Holzweg)*

The story goes that there used to be great paths cut through the forests in medieval times so that travellers and horses could venture through them without constantly smashing their faces into trees. Life was simpler back then. If your face wasn't about to hit a tree, you were going the right way. Easy. Then lumberjacks came along armed with an axe and an unhelpful profit incentive, and started cutting away trees alongside the path, just to swap those trees for money or sandwiches. The poor horses and travellers then started to notice these extra gaps in the forest, and assumed that the path was splitting. Sometimes they would take the wrong one, wandering deep into the forest, only to find a dead-end, sawdust and sandwich crumbs, or a note reading ›Dear Forest, I.O.U. 14 trees. Love, Friendly Insane Lumberjack Gunther.‹

Paradoxically since lumberjacks like Gunther actually want to be *on the woodway*, can they, in fact, be said to *be on the*

woodway? If a tree falls on the *woodway* and there is no one there to hear it, does it still make a sound? Yes, *woodways* are quite the brain teaser. Which is another good reason to avoid them, and while you're at it, those terrorists of forestry – lumberjacks. You just can't be too careful these days.

Ass Monkey Castle *(Aschaffenburg)*

There was an amazing story that went around the news in 2012. A sweet, elderly church-going grandmother tried to restore her village church's hundred-year-old painting of Jesus. The result mostly just looked like a face drawn on a thumb, except by someone who'd never seen a face or a thumb. It was incredible. One BBC correspondent said it looked like a »crayon sketch of a very hairy monkey in an ill-fitting tunic«. Another called it simply »potato Jesus«. Either way, what initially seemed like a disaster for the small Spanish village of 5000 people quickly turned into an internet sensation attracting an endless stream of delighted tourists who wanted to view it. The formula is clear: Silly nonsense = instant cash.

Further proof of concept can be found in the Austrian town of Fucking, which has its city signs stolen approximately three times a week by drunken English tourists.

So, while etymology might tell us that the city *Aschaffenburg* originally means »castle at the ash tree river«, deriving from the river *Aschaff* which runs through the town, we would like to suggest if the town's economy ever needs a quick boost from giggly tourists, they just hire that well-meaning Spanish grandmother to handpaint an *R* into all of the towns signs, write a quick e-mail to Lonely Planet, and begin the mega Denglisch tourist-trap »*Ass Monkey Castle*«.

I understand only train station
(Ich verstehe nur Bahnhof)

Germans are technical pioneers, deserving of their international recognition for mastery in engineering and logistics. In short, they thrive at complexity. Train stations are vital logistical hubs. While for German speakers, this expression usually means that of confusion, when abroad it could be repackaged to remind the *Ausländer* that even when you understand nothing of whatever boring thing they are saying, you still understand train stations. Rather than an expression of confusion, then, we'd suggest using it when you are bored or forced to engage in frivolous small talk. So, when a foreigner says »how are you?« when he doesn't know you, or tries to engage you in a discussion about the weather, reality TV, sporting results, or your feelings, answer »*I understand only train station.*« This is a gentle reminder that their topic is boring, you are both mortal, and they should return the conversation to something more intellectually stimulating.

World Room (*Weltraum*)

It can be scary to think about the sheer enormity of space. It can make one feel like a tiny, inadequate, cosmic dot. If English adopted the Denglisch *World Room*, however, perhaps we'd be far less intimidated by our insignificance. It's not space. It's not nothingness. It's just a big, old room. Sure, it's also the biggest room you could ever imagine. A room without a beginning or an end. A room lacking in atmosphere and *kipp*able windows. But, so what. Still a room. In the near future when we're all flying around in our personal spaceships, it's going to sound much scarier to say »I'm heading out into space«, rather than »I'm just nipping out to the *World Room* to pick us up some of that takeaway you like – you know, from that planet out by Globular Star Cluster 9. Won't be long.«

Wind Trousers *(Windhose)*

While at university, I experienced an earthquake. I'd like to tell you that experiencing an earthquake was very scary. That I acted heroically to save myself, and an attractive woman who quickly fell in love with me. And also a puppy with an injured leg and an eye patch. But sadly, real life is so rarely like the movies. No. Instead, I was sitting in the living room playing Mario Kart with my roommate Fraser. There was a slight rumble underfoot. I turned to Fraser and said, »Can you feel that?« He replied, »Can I feel what?« Then I said, »Oh, it's stopped now«. That was it. England doesn't really get proper earthquakes. In fact, we only knew there was an earthquake because it was the top story on the local news that evening. The epicenter had been a few miles away, and a street sign had been damaged. It was a big story. Unfortunately, I can't really tell people now that I've ›experienced an earthquake‹ because once I tell them this story, they say mean things like »that doesn't count«, »you're exaggerating« or »get out of my house, liar«. So what the English language and I need is a cute little diminutive word for earthquake that we can use, just like how the German language has *Wind Trousers* as a cute diminutive word for a tornado. »You call that a tornado, Holger? It's little more than a light *Wind Trousering*! Get back out there, you little *Fear Bunny*.«

Falling Umbrella Hunter *(Fallschirmjäger)*

One night, I was trying to read a book in German. This is very different to reading a normal book for me because I read it about eight times slower, it is eight times more painful, and requires my German girlfriend to be next to me, reading it as well then intermittently napping until I'm ready to turn the page. I remember the first time I stumbled upon the word *Fallschirmjäger*. I turned to her. »What's this long word, amongst all these other long words that are your language?,« I said. She leaned in towards the book. »You can figure that out. It's all there,« she encouraged, like an ever-kindly kindergarten teacher. I stared at the word. Studied it. Broke it down to its constituent parts. It was not »all there«. *A Falling Umbrella Hunter*? What? »If it is ›all there‹«, I asked her, »why am I now imagining an evil Mary Poppins, cackling insanely, flying through a stormy night with a black umbrella, singing spiteful songs, and hunting for children to poison with sweets?«

»Because you're stupid,« she replied.

Don't ask after sunshine
(Frag nicht nach Sonnenschein)

Most people in England don't go on holiday to experience the culture of other countries, but to experience somewhere *exactly* like England, except twelve degrees warmer. If the British Isles had a central thermostat that they could turn up to about 22 degrees Celsius, you would never see another Englishperson off their island ever again, except maybe for a World Cup or a war. So when booking a holiday, there is really only two important criteria the English ask after – »Will it be hotter than where I am now? And, if so, how do I get to the airplane?« The importing of the Denglisch expression *don't ask after sunshine* might be just the gentle nudge they need to remind them that there are other questions that could also be asked. Like about culture. History. Language. Architecture. A friendly reminder that holidays can sometimes be more than an opportunity to wear Union Jack swimming shorts, drink cheap cocktails, and eat egg-and-chips until you are alcohol-poisoned, grease-sodden, and sunburned enough to go home.

We sit quite beautifully in the ink
(Wir sitzen ganz schön in der Tinte)

Since the exact origin of this phrase is unclear, I'll gladly take this opportunity to wildly speculate. I think this idiom hints at a quiet fastidiousness in the German psyche. A rejection of that which is flashy and modern and fashionable, in favour of the timeless, regardless of its efficiency. Ink over digital. The letter over the e-mail. Handicraft over mass-produced. It says that, while the way we're doing it might not be the quickest, there's a beauty in doing it right, however slowly. It says, ›I don't care if the road is clear, because the *Ampelmännchen* is red. I don't care if University education fees in Germany are vastly lower than the European average, they're still too high. I don't care how long it takes to sort my rubbish into five bins, the *Umwelt* is worth it. I don't care about research that says electronic toys with movements and lights and sounds are more likely to stimulate my child, for I believe strongly in the educational superiority of wooden toys, shaped vaguely like an animal of some rough approximate description. If I'm wrong, I'm wrong. We'll all end up *sitting in the ink*, but we'll sit beautifully, because we're doing what we think is right.

I know that's actually the complete opposite of the saying, which is »now we're in trouble«, and that by merely suggesting this alternative origin I'm probably sitting down myself in all sorts of ink. But so be it. Here I will sit. Defiant. *Beautifully in the ink.*

My Dear Mister Singing Club's School of Denglisch: Doch, ja klar, äh nein, ich mein jein!

It's a proudly mooted (but largely unverified) fact that English has the most words of any world language, which is why it's so hard to believe we don't have something like the simple genius of German's *doch*. It's possibly because we're more a culture of argument avoiders, of agreeing to disagree, than Smart Shitter. Rather than *doch* our way back and forth to the most likely answer, we'd rather avoid the debate entirely by saying, »that's interesting that you think humans come from space eggs, I see where you are coming from, but let's *agree to disagree*.«

It's time for that to change. For us to stand up for ourselves. With Germany the heart of Europe, our economy struggling, our tourism reliant on a very old woman in London and all her palaces, and having been mocked by Vladimir Putin for being merely »a small island no one listens to«, we need a better, more forceful way to stand up for ourselves. We need *doch*. Germany, I propose a trade. The English language and the German language can meet in a secluded park, the English language will wear a bowler hat, and the German can carry a bouquet of *Spargel*. They'll both have briefcases, containing a word to trade. They'll sit on an empty bench. The English language will go first, nudging its briefcase across with its foot. They say nothing, avoid eye contact, swap, then stand up and leave in opposite directions, as fog swallows both their silhouettes and the sounds of their footsteps.

Later they open the briefcases and release their word hostages. The English find the word *doch* and rejoice, because we'll finally have a way to answer negatively phrased questions like »you don't really need the word *doch* in English, do you?«

»Yes.«

»Yes, you do? Or yes, you don't?«

»Yes, we do.«

»Need it or don't need it?«

»YES! YES! YES! WE REALLY NEED THE WORD *DOCH*: NOW SHUT UP AND HELP ME FIND MY BOWLER HAT, I'VE GOT TO MEET SOMEONE IN THE PARK!«

Yet when the Germans open their briefcase, they're immediately surprised. They assume there must have been some kind of confusion, because they find not one but two words! Hurrah! Then, on closer inspection, they realise they already had both those words. They were the words »mobile« and »phone«. *Mobile phone.* In a language so famed for soldering words together, they had never thought of this combination. They tried it on for size, rolled it around in the mouth, »mobile phone«. Not bad, not bad at all. It was a great day for the country of Germany, probably worthy of national holiday status – *Tag der Deutschen Neueinstufung*, to celebrate the day the nonsensical word *Handy* was finally put to rest.

As if the existence of *doch* hadn't already put English's binary system of answering questions to shame, innovative Germans have also invented *Jein* to mean yes and no simultaneously. It is an important distinction between the English equivalent answer, which would be the much faffier »well …

yes aaaand no …« When someone in England – the Mecca of Small Talkers – uses this expression, what they really mean is yes *or* no except, in addition, they are also going to waste a large portion of your day by not getting to the point first because they're afraid of being impolite, or want to grasp any opportunity to waffle needlessly.

For example, if someone asks an English person the rather simple question, »would you like to go for a walk?«, the reply, »well … yes aaaand no …« signals that you should sit down, take off your shoes, and get comfortable. It's faff time, island-style.

»Well … yes aaaaand no … I mean, it's a lovely day for a walk, I love the idea of it, yes, I mean, especially after all this rain we've been having recently. Can you believe this weather? I can't believe it just seems to do what it wants, just like weather always does. That reminds me, I went for a walk in 1974, and that had some weather too. Yellow, I believe, with a hint of breeze. I would love to go for that kind of walk again, yes, and I suppose this walk you're proposing now could be that kind of walk, yes. I mean, anything is possible, right, on a nice walk? Ahhh, yes – unfortunately, I'll have to say no, as I lost my legs this morning in a shark attack.«

In German, however, they would just get to the point.

»Want to go for a walk?«

»Jein. Nice day. No legs. Schönen Tag noch.«

Denglisch Food and Drink

In its shortness lay its spice

Adjusting to the eating habits of a new culture can sometimes be difficult. There are famous examples of where asking for more is seen as very polite or completely rude. In Germany, the main problems come with adjusting to the durations and quantities of the food. First, there is the breakfast, where the emphasis is much more on the *break*, than the *fast*. Eating, talking, reading, thinking, eating some more, talking, smoking, drinking coffee, eating, napping, eating, etc. In a culture that is world-famous for efficiency, the German breakfast is an area of life where one feels there might still be space for some optimisation.

Main meals tend to be of the simple variety. Generally, they just involve killing a large animal and laying it whole across everyone's plates. Alongside it will be an over abundance of, or, some might say, an over-reliance on – the potato, apple of the earth. There's very little a German can't do with an *Earth Apple*. But mostly they'll just keep serving it to you, no matter what you order. It may start to feel like you were not invited to a dinner party, but instead, a carb riot. *Prosting* will occur often. Then, once it's all over and you've had your love life for the next seven years categorised as either ›carry on as normal‹ or ›get worse‹, your waiter gets both *Drink Money* and a public maths exam in the form of *Split Bill* before everyone bikes home.

Dinner is usually a simple *Evening Bread* affair, and for a reason unknown to all, tends to be served on a wooden board. This serves a dual purpose, firstly it holds food, as in the timeless tradition of a plate, and, secondly, if the food is not to your tastes, you can carve a message of disappointment to the chef, or, if you are the chef, a very tiny canoe.

To come in the devil's kitchen
(In Teufels Küche kommen)

What exactly is in the devil's kitchen that Germans are so afraid of? Why when they're in trouble do they liken themselves to being *in the devil's kitchen*? Would that actually be such a bad thing? The devil is used to cooking. He's mingled with the evil chefs of every culture. The devil's kitchen would have the finest ovens, and a completely bitching array of spices with the flames set to singe. I'm imagining the devil in there, in his Kiss the Cook apron, knocking up quite literally the omelette from hell, pausing occasionally to add several dashes of paprika, chilli, or a splash of eternal damnation. He'd bring some flair and charisma to the tired world of German cuisine. A world in which, regardless of the question, for years the answer has always been »add some *Senf*«.

Luck Mushroom *(Glückspilz)*

Being a full-time idiot, I only know one thing about mushrooms, which is that full-time idiots shouldn't go out in the woods picking mushrooms and eating them if they only know one thing about mushrooms. Indeed, because I don't know which ones are edible, which ones kill you, and which ones personally introduce you to god, my very survival is dependent on me going to a supermarket to buy them picked and idiot-proofed for me by professionals and machines. Presumably, the Denglisch *Luck Mushroom* came from a person exactly like me. Maybe a naive foreigner who once accompanied a group of eager, hiking Germans into a wood to pick mushrooms, naively ate everything they found, and yet still lived to tell the tale.

Mirror Egg *(Spiegelei)*

When you really, really think about it, an egg is a bit like a mirror. Maybe even the truest, most profound mirror of all. For what the egg reflects is not man or egg, but the very universe itself – creation, oneness, rebirth, the infinite continuation of life begetting life, the passage of time in cause and consequence, and all contained within its own self-sustaining universe. Wow.

Of course, when you really, really think about it, you might also realise that you are really, really thinking about it too much. Such is the deep, mystical power of the *Mirror Egg*, a breakfast reflection of your soul. However, while the *Mirror Egg* seems to want »breakfast-eaters« to ask themselves the ultimate question, ›who am I?‹, they are still less confusing in the morning than *Lost Eggs (verlorene Eier)*, which are more likely to beg the question, ›what do you mean they're lost? Where did they go? I'm hungry.‹

Over liquid *(Überflüssig)*

In cheesy movies about American Football, it is not uncommon to hear some intensely deranged coach screaming at his fresh team of plucky young underdogs to »GO OUT THERE AND GIVE ME 110 PERCENT!!«

Somehow, the muscular dullards seem encouraged, presumably because their speciality is not maths, but running into each other like huge lumps of armour-wrapped ham. The same battle cry would not work for Germans, who are brought up with the embedded wisdom that any liquid that does not fit correctly in the container is pointless. 100 percent fits in the container. 110 percent is water on the bathroom floor. Beer on the bar. Tsunami on the power plant.

»No, Mr Coach,« the wise Denglischman replies, »you shall only get 100 percent of my effort until you buy a second container in which to put it. *A good horse jumps only as high as it must*. Anything more is just *over liquid*.«

I don't trust that roast
(Ich trau dem Braten nicht)

This expression is from an old fable about a farmer who invites one of his pigs to his house for dinner. The animal, though apparently smart enough to receive and action a dinner invitation, was unfortunately not smart enough to remember his main role in the hierarchy of the farm here in Germany, the land of the sausage. He happily accepts the invitation. However, as the pig gets closer to the kitchen, he starts to smell what is roasting, and the smell of what is roasting is strangely familiar. Recognisable, somehow. He can't quite put his hoof on it. Actually, it smells a bit like that time his Uncle Monty burnt his tail in the small, but now legendary barn fire of 1998.

Then the pig has two quick awkward realisations in a row: »That smell is pig …wait … *I'm a pig*!« He figures out that it's a trap, then runs away, or gets eaten, or something. I can't remember the end. Come to think of it, it might not have been a pig at all. Might have been a cow, or a goose, or a hare, or a horse. What's important is the sentiment, which is that it's very easy to go from being life's distinguished guest, to being life's main course. *Don't trust that roast.*

With me is not good cherries eating
(Mit mir ist nicht gut Kirschen essen)

Let's say we set up an internationally recognised scale to measure the scariness of verbal threats, like the Richter scale, or that one with voltage that no one ever remembers. At the top of this new scale, we could put an Italian mob boss threatening to send you to sleep with the fishes, or putting a horse's head in your bed. Or if that's still not scary enough, how about a drunken, toothless Glaswegian saying, »Are you talking to me or are you chewing a brick? Because either way you're going to lose your teeth!«

While I don't want to be disrespectful, I'd like to suggest that at the absolute opposite end of this new verbal danger scale would have to be the German threat *with me is not good cherries eating.* Allowing myself an understatement, I'd say it sounds slightly limp. Is it actually a threat? An irrelevant fact shared by someone who doesn't like cherry eating? Or both? In a way this makes it the perfect Denglisch challenge. Like a bank robber armed with only a pocket and a banana, we challenge you to bluff threaten someone, armed only with the expression *with me is not good cherries eating.* Success is if instead of *laughing themselves dead*, they twitch like the little *Fear Bunnies* that they are.

My Dear Mister Singing Club's School of Denglisch: Du you Sie me?

Most days now, I wake up to a visit from Peter. He lives opposite me in Berlin, and I suspect is an alcoholic. This is partly because he often asks if I want to come over for a whiskey. Mostly, though, it's because he often asks if I want to come over for a whiskey before I've even had muesli.

Over the course of our friendship, Peter has taught me many a thing, most of which relate to swearing, drinking, and hitting me on the arm. Perhaps the most important thing he has taught me, though, is not always to befriend your neighbours.

German has a wonderful system for separating formal and informal relationships, and it is as easy to *Sie* as it is to *Du*. Ho ho ho.

I ignored it.

Unfortunately, when I first met Peter, or as I should have been calling him *Herr Decker*, I naively went in all-smiles-blazing, du-du-dee-du-dee-du, inviting him full force into the friend category. Five minutes later, he was at my door with a handful of shot glasses, two bottles of whiskey, and a photograph of himself holding an assault rifle that he wanted photocopied, by me, his new best friend.

Ho ho oh … my … god.

At the time, I didn't know the rules of when to use *Du* and when to use *Sie*. Now that I think about it, I still don't. Sure, sometimes it's obvious. Old people, bosses, teachers, fine. But it's the nuances of it that confuse me: what if I get drunk with my boss, and he suggests I call him ›*Du*‹ after two glasses of wine? Do I dare risk the *Du* with him in the sober-light of morning? What do you say to a police officer if he is arresting you but is also your son? What do you call yourself when you travel back in time? What if I get drunk with my boss, and go back in time to arrest myself, but get amnesia and forget that he's my father?

Wait. Hold on. I've got a bit confused.

Either way, it's obviously an issue that could cause a lot of potential problems, especially when you're overly imaginative.

Coming from English – the only Indo-European language to discard its separate forms of ›you‹ – it was initially a very strange concept for me. Why do I have to decide when and if someone is younger than me? Why do I have to decide if someone is above or beneath me?

WHY CAN'T WE ALL JUST GET ALONG?!

Then I realised that *Du* and *Sie* might have very real, practical uses. Like with Peter my neighbour. If he became too troublesome to deal with, I could switch back to ›*Sie*‹ to distance myself from him until he got the message. The next day, he would forget, and we would use ›*Du*‹ again. It became like a cycle, whereby whether I was using ›*Du*‹ or ›*Sie*‹ was roughly in accordance with the time of day, how much he'd had to drink, and how much patience I had to talk to him. Peter still comes round most days, to ask for some money, give me an odd little gift that he's not legally obtained, to ask if I'll have a drink with him, or to ask if I can do a »goo-glee« for something.

I should have been firmer in my *Sies* from the outset. But you don't need to make that same mistake, you still have at your disposal an old and powerful gift – one meaning, two purposes. ›*Du*‹ says, »come in, my friend, borrow my house shoes, make yourself at home, let's catch a movie later, or share a deli-cooked chicken.«

›*Sie*‹ says, »stay there,« and closes the door.

Denglisch Mind and Body

Helping hold your ears stiff

I had my first German cold this year, and it was wonderful. I used to get English colds fairly regularly, and they were rubbish. You just had to get on with your life, except with a cough and a runny nose. You looked a bit worse, felt a bit worse, and people avoided you slightly more than usual.

I didn't even know the common cold was different in other countries until I came to Germany. I woke up one morning with a cough and a slight sniffle. I tried to get up to go to work, but my girlfriend pushed me back down.

Germans are amazing during times of sickness. They're part mother, part *sicksisters*, part pharmacist, and part dispenser of mystical German wisdom. Normal life shuts down. Your cold is your life now.

»No, it's alright,« I said, »it's just a cold.«

»No, you can't possibly do anything today!,« she said.

I was going to argue, until I realised what I was arguing against. She wanted me to stay in bed all day while she bought me food and hot drinks, and I was arguing to go to work. Was I insane? I decided to trust her, not my health, and indulge my cold. It was amazing. She immediately wrapped the magic *German scarf of ultimate healing* around my neck, then went out and brought back half an *Apotheke*. Stuff went on my chest, up my nose, down my throat, and I *hedgehoged myself* in a duvet all day while she gave me endless ginger-lemon-honey-magic-tea potions. Now, so keen am I to get sick again and return to this magical German Wellness Narnia that I've started licking public transportation seats, paying people to sneeze on me and only leaving the house when I have wet hair and bare feet.

Feel somebody on the tooth
(Jemandem auf den Zahn fühlen)

I once saw a performance from a magician, in which he sat people down and just talked about tooth pain, until after a few minutes, they all had it and were either leaving or begging him to stop. I found the whole thing implausible and guessed they must be actors. That was until I got my first letter from the *Finanzamt*. Telling me I didn't fill out a big-long-word and I now needed to do this other-long-word or another giant-german-legal-threat-thing was going to happen and I wouldn't want that because of some bullet points. I immediately felt a sharp pain in my teeth. This now happens every time I open a letter and see the word *Finanzamt*. You could say, much like that magician, the *Finanzamt* are also very good at *feeling somebody on the tooth*.

Secret Advice Corner *(Geheimratsecke)*

It's not unusual to read about indigenous tribes that have elaborate coming-of-age ceremonies in which boys become men by heading out into the woods to complete a feat of skill and courage, whether that is killing an antelope with their bare hands or climbing a sacred, haunted mountain. In any civilised culture, a man losing his hair could be deserving of similar reverence. It is also a rite of passage, from naive vanity to worldly humbleness. A new stage in the journey of manhood. A stage that, admittedly, will mostly just consist of anxiety and wearing hats. But it's a new stage, nonetheless. No, sir, he's not »going bald«. He's not a »cue ball«. He's not

»gaining head«, you cheeky little *Fun Bird*. The German language understands this. It respects it. It makes it positive. He's cultivating *Secret Advice Corners*, where his knowledge and wisdom can quietly multiply.

Anti Baby Pill *(Antibabypille)*

The English language has become increasingly blasé about one of the most revolutionary medicines in the modern world. Originally called the »combined oral contraceptive pill«, it wasn't long before we were calling it just the »birth control pill«. Eventually, we were so relaxed about it; it just became »the pill«. Just the pill. Like we'd forgotten that we'd just rewired millions of years of biological evolution with a handful of tablets, and were now free to bump uglies with whoever we wanted without the lifelong consequences of children. Presumably it was around this time that England achieved the dubious honour of highest teenage pregnancy rate in Western Europe, with confused girls thinking anything called the pill could be taken sporadically whenever there was a vaguely pill-worthy symptom. Headaches. Belly ache. Sneezing. So, in order to combat this problem, the English should adopt the no-nonsense German word *Anti Baby Pill*. Its blunt sentiment sits you down, tells you off, and then launches into a two hour lecture about responsibility. Nothing could be less romantic. Nothing could dampen a raging teenage libido more effectively. It's like a condom for the mind.

To be washed with all waters
(Mit allen Wassern gewaschen sein)

Once upon a time, sailors used to travel the seven seas, learning the hard ways of the world, getting older, tougher, wiser, finding treasure, getting scurvy, adopting a parrot, having adventures, literally washing in all of the world's waters. Unfortunately, no one sails these days. Instead, most prefer arguing with discount airlines about the size of their backpack and its contents. We've gone from washing with all waters, to carrying a maximum of 100ml. So let's reserve this little Denglisch gem for the true, modern equivalent of that seafaring, life-learning adventuring sailor. Someone that is still learning life's lessons the hard way. Someone, that with respect to liquids, has not quite found their appropriate limit. The guy passed out in the corner of the bar, hugging his barstool at 7pm with toilet roll hanging out of his jeans. The young group of girls mixing drinks, and chanting »shots, shots, shots!« as if personal friends with ethanol, blissfully unaware how much tomorrow will hurt. Gin, Vodka, Beer, Jagerbombs. They're *washing with all waters* as well, except with one crucial difference: now they're on the inside, polishing their livers.

Sitting Pee-er *(Sitzpinkler)*

Ignoring the few minor areas of politics, religion, work, and golf, everyone knows it's better to be a woman than a man. No one ever asks you to kill a spider. You never have to pretend you like sports. You live longer. You can have multiple orgasms.

In fact, the only obvious advantage of being a man these days is that you can pee standing up, and therefore, just about anywhere. To give up this great privilege of nature, as many German men have, shows great courage. An acknowledgement, that while it's better for you to pee standing up, it's worse for everyone else. To not do it shows you're a team player with a willingness to blur the gender lines. Someone who would gladly stay up late and talk about their feelings. Someone who is not ashamed to admit crying at the end of »Toy Story 3«. You're a *sitting Pee-er* and Germany salutes you – or rather Germany's girlfriends and wives salute you – although they all still also reserves the right to mock you behind your back for being wimpy by calling you »*a sitting Pee-er*«. Ignore them, brave modern man.

My Dear Mister Singing Club's School of Denglisch: Shitstorm

As with any foreign language, one of the first and early joys is learning how to swear. You instantly revert back to the mindset of a child – you say the words, you giggle, you know you're being naughty, but you don't quite know why. This is because using foreign swear-words doesn't have the natural effect on you that it does for native speakers, who have had a lifetime of context, conditioning and chastisement. To everyone else, they're just noises. So I hope you'll excuse me in this chapter if I use German swear-words a little more freely than a normally polite book should.

Generally, you should learn swear-words before you can count to five, or pronounce basic verbs like »to be« or »to go.« When I started learning German, for instance, I quickly gained the ability to lose all of my friends before I had the language skills to make any.

Perhaps I was hanging around with the wrong crowd, but I knew three words for »shit« before I even knew the word »three«. Really. With great delight, I was taught about *Stuhl*, which you learn quickly when you want to find a chair with the wrong friends, *Scheiße*, perhaps the most generous word in all of German, and *Durchfall* – my favourite word in all of the language so far, being as it was my introduction to the joy of compounding, the clarity of mental imagery on offer in the

German language, and the complete, romance-less precision of Denglisch.

»Fall through.«

Indeed.

Soon after, I was making joking references to German speakers about the fact that I had »learned three words for ›shit‹, before I learned the word ›three‹!« The response to this statement, incidentally, was never that anybody would teach me the word »drei«, but lots more words for »shit«.

When learning languages with such an incredibly dumb theme, it isn't long into German that the pervasiveness of *Scheiße* starts to become apparent. In 2013, they even added another form of it when the Duden controversially included Anglicism »shitstorm« for the first time. Indeed, Angela Merkel's recent use of the word »shitstorm« had caused quite a shitstorm itself in the foreign press. Heads of State are allowed to swear, they asked? In a press conference? Indeed, just about the only place it didn't cause a shit storm was in Germany, where nobody even knew it was supposed to be a swear-word in the first place, and didn't really understand all the fuss about a little storm of shit.

It was only once German started to import other language's words for »shit« that I started to wonder if there was some truth in the long-standing rumour that the language was obsessed with the stuff. Not an original thought, and something actually researched by real life linguists. Indeed, one by the name of Hans-Martin Gauger spent several years comparing swear-words in 15 different languages and concluded it's not that Germans are obsessed with faecal matters, as often suggested, but rather, they prefer not to use sexual metaphors in negative sentiments like many other languages. Which makes really a lot of sense. Why demonise something as healthy and natural as sex?

When I delicately brought up the theme of swearing with my German friends, they would ask me the same thing: why is English swearing so obsessed with sex and the genitals, particularly focusing on synonyms for the penis?

»Is there something wrong with genitals?« they asked me.

»No, of course not,« I replied.

»Do you think children should grow up to be afraid of their bodies? To think that one part of them is specifically offensive, or bad, or wrong, and should not be freely displayed on the FKK-friendly beaches of their country?«

»Well, no.«

»And is there something wrong with sex?«

»Well, no.«

»Do you think children should grow up to think sex is a wrong, dirty thing, instead of a normal, healthy act of free expression between two people? That when it is talked about, it should be in hushed tones? That we should stigmatise it as something other than a normal and necessary bodily act?«

»Well, no.«

»Do you think shit stinks?«

»Well … err … yes?«

»Good. Welcome to Germany.«

Denglisch and Animals

It thinks it kicks a horse!

I would like to make a tentative suggestion, one that perhaps only as ignorant a foreigner as me could make: Germany chose the wrong national animal.

Now, I'm not complaining about the *Adler*. That's one nice looking bird. The problem as I see it is that if you gathered a representative from every country in the world, and asked them »which country's national animal is the eagle?«, every single country other than Germany is going to respond »America.«

Obviously, that's not Germany's fault. America's marketing team was just more prolific, going all around the world, as it did, inviting itself straight into people's living rooms via Hollywood, and spreading itself around via its overly-enthusiastic foreign policy. Regardless of how it happened, though, the German national animal is ripe for a re-brand.

Luckily for Germany, while the milk-giving cow has become the symbol of several countries, the pig remains mysteriously unclaimed. That's right, don't eat the *Grief Bacon* just yet, the pig remains unclaimed! And what a fine and fitting animal it would be, forming as it does so much of the German language.

My first introduction to the cultural weightiness of the pig was unfortunately a bit of a disappointing one. When I first moved in with my German girlfriend, we were talking about how we could save a little money for a while. Unfortunately, I misheard her, and thought that her suggestion was that we get a *Spaßswine*, a fun pig. I love pigs. Especially fun ones. So, despite not quite understanding what economic benefits were on offer, I was far too delighted with the idea to question her. Imagine my disappointment when she came home with a *Sparswine*. I mean, it's OK, but it's not as fun to play with in the garden as I had hoped.

The longer I stayed in Germany, however, the more I realised the unlikelihood I would ever be allowed to have a pig as a pet, considering how constantly the poor, clever beast's name is used to insult people. It seems to me that you can put the word »swine« on the end of any noun, and it becomes immediately insulting. »*Käseschwein*«, »*Froschschwein*«, »*Versicherungschwein*«, etc. You don't have to say yes right now, but just think on it a little, will ya? *Betrachtungschwein*. Great. In the meantime we'll take a little wander through the entertaining world of Denglisch Animals.

Over Monkey Horny *(Oberaffengeil)*

There are several videos on the internet of monkeys sexually assaulting frogs. I watch them sometimes. Some people, let's call them normal people to help us identify them, may find such videos offensive and unsuitable viewing for the work lunch break. To these people I say *pppfffffff*. These videos are perfect for when you're feeling particularly smug and highly evolved. After an evening setting the world to rights. After being lectured on the futility of everything by a nihilist. Or reading about another school in America that's also forcing its teachers to teach creationism. When I see that little monkey leaning back, a big grin on his face, working away with his frog, I see only the single most convincing argument for Darwin's Theory of Evolution imaginable. This is why we need the expression *over monkey horny*. We're animals. We came from chimps. We get horny. It's cool. Get over it.

Donkey Bridge *(Eselsbrücke)*

The English language has no poetic equivalent of *Eselsbrücke*. It has »mnemonic« and »memory aid«. »Mnemonic« is, rather ironically, a very unmemorable word. A flamboyant combination of M and N, tripping up both speakers and spellers. »Memory aid«, meanwhile, sounds like the kind of vitamin supplement you might see on offer in your e-mail's spam folder. But *Donkey Bridge?! Donkey Bridge!* Perfect. Saddle whatever you want to know on the back of your trusty memory steed, he'll easily carry the weight of whatever needs

94

remembering. Looking up at you, your Memory Donkey says, »Relax. I got this. Over we go. Over the *Donkey Bridge* to Memoryville. I won't let you down.«

Ear Worm *(Ohrwurm)*

There's a grass roots campaign in England (okay, I'm exaggerating slightly but comedian Stephen Fry did once sent a tweet about it) to try and introduce the German concept of *Ear Worms* into the English language. At present, English lacks any succinct way to label this curious phenomenon. Of the worst song from the pub playing endlessly in your head, on a continuous, repetitive loop, replacing cherished thoughts and memories with Boney M or the Village People, or not being able to sleep because »I'm blue da ba dee da ba daa« is busy burrowing itself into your brain. According to the inter-

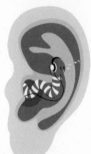

I'm Blue
da ba dee da ba daa
da ba dee da ba daa
da ba dee da ba da
da ba dee da ba ...

net, the best English can currently do is »musical imagery repetition« and »involuntary musical imagery«, neither of which quite encapsulate the burrowing, annoying and un-invited nature of the problem. Like a burglar, only for the mind, who not only refuses to leave, but insists on standing directly in front of you and jiggling, while loudly humming the chorus to your absolute least favourite song. Except it isn't the whole chorus, that would be something. The evil *Ear Worm* is not usually so kind. It just takes the song, smashes it up, glues random parts back together again, adding some of its own personal suggestions, until you're stuck humming a misguided mish-mash of vaguely similar-sounding non-sense, like »Sometimes I feel, boom boom! Paaaainted love! Boom boom! Paaaainted love! Get awaaaay. Boom boom!«

Fear Bunny *(Angsthase)*

The fact that the English language uses the expression »scaredy-cat« to refer to someone who is afraid of something might lead you to the conclusion that the English language has never had a serious altercation with a cat. Cats have teeth. Cats have claws. Cats are fast. Springy. Agile. Decisive. Ruthless. You can pick up a cat, spin it round your head like a furry meat propeller, then throw it as hard as you can from a 100-storey high building. This will not bother the cat. This will not upset the cat. The cat will land gently, look at you, then carry on with its day as if it hadn't even noticed. You are nothing to a cat. No one. They're fearless feline warriors. »Scaredy-cat« is an inappropriate use of language, and must be replaced immediately with Denglisch's fluffy, cuddly, *Fear Bunny*. An animal whose primary defence methods are twitching its nose and playing dead.

Tie a bear on someone
(Jemandem einen Bären aufbinden)

According to my thorough and in-depth research, the origin of this phrase goes a little like this: Once upon a time, there were some hunters who went to a tavern for some food and drinks. Unfortunately, they didn't have any money. »Don't worry, though,« they said to the pub's landlord, »while we may not have money now, we do have a nice bear to prove our status as upstanding gentlemen of an honest persuasion. We shall tie him outside as a deposit for our food and drinks. We will return later, of course, to collect him and settle our debts.« Being German, of course, the pub accepted this offer. For it was a *pfand-tastic* proposal. The hunters ate and drank everything they wanted, ran up the biggest bar tab they could, shots all round, everyone, and one for you Mr Barkeeper, then ran away without paying. »Haha, jokes on you,« said the pub, »… we have your bear!« It was only at this point that the pub realised it didn't need a bear, because pubs generally don't need bears, because pubs are pubs. »Oh«, said the pub. »Damn.«

Since then, as a reminder of this I'll-just-leave-my-bear-here-and-I'll-be-right-back scam, the German language has retained the expression *to tie a bear on someone*, meaning to trick, and also, presumably, for when someone really is trying to tie a bear onto you. Admittedly, this doesn't seem to happen all that often here, but would almost be worth it for the chance to say »are you tying a bear on me in order to tie a bear on me?«

Spike Pig *(Stachelschweine)*

Sigmund Freud once popularised the idea of the hedgehog's or porcupine's dilemma. He compared the emotional nature of human ~~sex~~ relationships to that of spiked animals wanting to huddle up for ~~penis~~ ~~mother~~ warmth. Sure, you want to be close to each other, to be more intimate, to bask in each other's body heat, but the closer you get, the more you will always inevitably hurt each other. It's a beautiful and sad idea. ~~Daddy never loved me~~. It seems to challenge us before any first date: shall I risk everything like the *Spike Pig*, or stay home and safely *hedgehog myself*? Thus, we suggest, *Spike Pig* be adopted as a label we give to the brave, for people who leave the house in inappropriate footwear, without a plan, a map, people who holiday in exotic lands without any chance of a humble *Schorle*. People who start *Vereins*. People who shout their way through every *Ruhetag*. Chant through every protest. Scream through every handball match. Dance and sing to every *Schlager* hit. People who stand up for what they believe in, even if, tragically, they might end up popping that thing like it's a child's balloon. »Death or glory!« shouts the fearless *Spike Pig*.

Old foxes go hard into the trap
(Alte Füchse gehen schwer in die Falle)

It is perhaps due to the wisdom in old fashioned proverbs like this, that Germany has emerged as the strongest economy in Europe. While other European countries' younger foxes wandered naively into cheap, flashy traps set by their cash-happy, over-spending banks and governments, Germany stayed with what they knew. While others ran head-first into buying homes, and then second homes, and then third homes as »investments«, to rent to other people, then had to get credit cards, and then second credit cards, and then third credit cards to pay for the upkeep of those first, second and third homes, the Germans stayed faithful. They sniffed around the traps; remained sceptical; distrusting of the promises of quick easy profit, and signs that said »FREE CHICKENS – PUT YOUR FACE IN HERE!« They kept renting. They kept their finances in the black. They kept taking their beer bottles back to the supermarket to collect their €0,08 each. Now, while all others are in chaos, trapped, it is they who are prospering. Because like a nation of old foxes, Germany *goes hard into the trap*.

FREE
CHICKEN *
· 0% INTEREST
· AVAILABLE TODAY
· NO MONEY DOWN

* COOL YOUNG FOXES PREFERRED

Egglaying Wool Milk Pig
(Eierlegende Wollmilchsau)

I can only conclude that because the German language calls a generalist an *egglaying Wool Milk Pig,* it assumes such a humble animal would just muddle by with its slightly confused medley of meagre talents. Doing the best it can. I would beg to differ. I would even accuse the German language of vastly underestimating just how supreme and invincible an *egglaying Wool Milk Pig* would be. Were it to exist, it would surely become supreme overlord of all the animal kingdom, humbling the Lion to that of assistant regional manager. For what does the *egglaying Wool Milk Pig* lack? Nothing! What's that? What did you say? »Defences?« You think it lacks *defences*? That in a fight to the death with an eagle or a crocodile, it's egg-laying, wool-growing, milk-producing abilities would not be sufficient?

Nonsense.

Rich and powerful nations have been built on gold, cotton, tea, silk, opium, diamonds. Well, the *egglaying Wool Milk Pig,* with such bountiful natural resources at its disposal, in the form of the cute gift hampers full of milkshakes, omelettes and woollen socks it could offer, would easily be able to barter for the loyalties of more specialised, ferocious animals like bears or jackals. Really, Disney, that blockbuster hit should have been The Lion *egglaying Wool Milk Pig* King.

My Dear Mister Singing Club's School of Denglisch: Gender Surrender

I think probably every German language learner, at least if their native language doesn't have genders, is initially very excited by the idea of them. They dangle the idea of logic in front of us. We've always tacitly known that Bananas, Carrots and Asparagus are obviously masculine. Because, well, look at them. We know there is a lot of work to do, but one day there will be a new layer of understanding, depth and clarity to our messy cluttered lives.

We crack our knuckles, sharpen our pencils, open up our *German for Dumb Ausländer* text-books and then begin the actual process of memorising the genders. It's at this point that all the wheels fall off the wagon. Or, perhaps more accurately, they don't so much as fall off, but we rip them off in an angry disbelieving rant, after learning that the genders are, for the most part, just randomly assigned nonsense. Banana is not even male. I mean, really. You're looking for poetry where really there is mostly just perfunctory.

This is the part where ordinarily, to keep with the format of the rest of the book, I'd now argue that we should add genders into the English language. That's not an easy sell. Of course it would make the language much denser and would add a certain kind of poetry to it, which could be construed as a positive thing. *Der Mond*, *die Sonne*, the beautiful couple, dancing in the dark, doing the grand, cosmic waltz of night and day in the great dancehall of our sky.

Sounds good, doesn't it?

But since Old English had genders (even more illogically, in Old English a woman was masculine) and modern English still flirts with them from time to time, whether it's steward and stewardess, actor and actress, with certain countries like England being female, ships being »shes« and »hers«, etc., I'd be arguing against some wise forefather of mine, who had the wisdom to give genders the heave-ho from English.

English is distancing itself from genders. Chairman is becoming chairperson. Policeman is now police officer. Fireman, firefighter. We know we're supposed to do this, but we still tend to slack off and default back. So it's probably far too late for us to change and reintroduce genders. Plus, how would it work logistically? Would there be a nationwide referendum? Where at country level we could all vote on which gender to assign to the word »hermaphrodite«? No one would get anything done. We could make it a sort of televised lottery, a woman in a figure-hugging dress would smile and announce »tonight's noun is *ventriloquist*«, then a lottery machine full of balls denoting the three genders would whir into life, spit out the ball »*das*«, and that would be the gender of ventriloquist from now on.

Of course, the mistake we're making with German genders is in looking for clues in the object to enlighten us to its gender. We really want to personify everything. To put little dresses on female nouns like the cat, make-up on a mouse, trousers on a dog. Rather than understanding that the gender is merely a label, applied based on the word itself. Not the object the word represents. Once you know that, once you've learnt that *-heit*, *-keit*, *-schaft* and *-ung* are almost always female. That *-ling*, *-en*, *-er* and *-ich* are male, you can relax and enjoy what genders bring to the German language – hilarious mishaps. Like the man who went to buy a pet and came back not with a pony (*das Pony*), but with a new fringe (*der Pony*). That Mousse (*Mus*) is suffering an identity crisis and is neutral, female and male. Or the Turkish car salesman who was catapulted into stardom and surging car sales figures when he mistakenly referred to one of his vehicles as »*Der Gerät*« instead of »*Das Gerät*«. He was later invited to a major TV show just to repeat his little grammatically erotic blunder (and over a million people have watched it on You-Tube!).

Sometimes it feels to me like the German language operates on the same principle as the card game Mao, in which Germans staunchly attest that there are rules, but won't tell you them just for the fun of watching you say amusing, stupid things.

Denglisch Wisdom

Who won't listen must feel

Germans do not need to defend their language. They know that their language is the key to the ultimate store of age old knowledge. It will not be shared cheaply. There is no shortcut to enlightenment. Wisdom must be earned. German has timelessly proven itself almost beyond reproach in the fields of philosophy, literature, everything, and poetry. It's the language of Bach, Nietzsche, Kant, Marx, Goethe and many other equally important dead people who said smart things everyone is still trying to understand all these years later.

So, it's no surprise that this was the hardest chapter to put together, because we couldn't decide between so many great, smart expressions and amusing tongue twisters. Whether that of *holy Indian-honour-word (heiliges Indianerehrenwort), that went in the trousers (das ging in die Hose), he who fries someone else's sausage has a sausage-frying-device (Wer andern eine Bratwurst brät, der hat ein Bratwurst-Bratgerät), sometimes even blind chickens can also find corn (selbst ein blindes Huhn findet manchmal ein Korn), well-known like a colorful dog (bekannt wie ein bunter Hund),* or *to everywhere your mustard add (überall seinen Senf dazugeben).*

Sadly, in the end we've had to decide on just the following six entries.

Remember, you're going to die
(Bedenke, dass du sterben musst)

Young people have now bastardised the English phrase »you only live once«, to the shorter, poppier acronym *YOLO* which they text, tweet and shout as they run around doing a whole range of idiotic and mostly pointless things that endanger their health or at least their genitals. The phrase has become rocket fuel for reckless stupidity. For getting inside bins and rolling down hills. For prematurely practising parkour on rooftops and balconies. For chest-bumping shop windows. The no-nonsense, slightly old-fashioned German expression *»remember, you're going to die«* carries no such foolish bravado. It'll ground us all once again. Keep us humble. Because, it focuses not so much on the joy of living, but on the absolute certainty of death. The great downer. It says: »You will die, little Timmy, and soon, and possibly right this very second unless you come down from the roof. You can't fly. Those aren't wings. They're my old curtains, you flappy little dimwit.«

Is it art – or can I chuck it?
(Ist das Kunst – oder kann das weg?)

London has an art gallery called The Tate Modern. It is big, and contains art. It also contains rubbish. Sometimes the rubbish looks like art. Sometimes the art looks like rubbish. Sometimes the rubbish is art, and the art is rubbish. It's all very modern. Inside the right room, for example, an old, unmade bed can be celebrated, win prestigious prizes, then sell for hundreds of thousands of euros. Outside the building, however, and it would be begrudgingly removed by large resentful men in a lorry, at the cost of the taxpayer. The point of the wonderful, pretentiousness-challenging Denglisch expression »*Is it art – or can I chuck it?*« is a direct and quite German reminder to artists that if they're going to make »art« that is even vaguely confusable with rubbish, they must also justify why it is allowed to stay inside art galleries with the impressive paintings, and not be outside getting urinated on by a cat.

Live like god in France
(Leben wie Gott in Frankreich)

Germany's love of France needs no introduction. The country's attraction to Paris is historically well-documented. Perhaps this expression hints at why. As a comedy writer, of course, I don't like to use national stereotypes. *Ahem.* If I did, however, I would very much have to agree with the German assessment that the ultimate goal in life is to be all-knowing and all-powerful, yet in the land of the croissant. You'd eat breakfast at lunch, smoke a carton of cigarettes, drink a bottle of wine, grow a moustache, invent the universe, philosophise about the pointlessness of the universe, have sex all afternoon, then call an end to the work day at 3pm. What could be better than that? *Viva la D'anglais.*

Everything has an ending, only the sausage has two
(Alles hat ein Ende, nur die Wurst hat zwei)

The most inquisitive of foreigners is unlikely to accept this fact as true, a little because they are stubborn, but mostly because it's, well, not. If you use this expression and they reply with something like, »yeah, well, by that kind of simple logic, anything tubular also has two endings then, doesn't it? Toothpaste. Curtain Rails. Bananas. Those little dogs, what are they called? Ah yeah, *Dachshunds*.« If this happens, you should just march off dramatically, turning back only to proclaim »you just don't get it, do you!« or »oh, *Dachshunds* – another perfect example of another brilliant German word we lent your inferior language! And we don't even use it. Ha!«

Life is not a pony farm
(Das Leben ist kein Ponyhof)

Germans are not susceptible to frivolous, childish delusions like *utopia*. They know that the closest you could get to true happiness in this indifferent universe would be the job of pony farming. Just imagine! Every day, you get up early, prepare food for all the ponies, feed them all, take them all out, exercise them all, feed them all again, brush them all, then get a shovel and use it to remove great clumps of their stinky poop from the stables and your legs, then feed them again, then more brushing, more pooing, more feeding, more exercising, then you put all your clothes in the washing, try to get the smell off yourself, go to bed, then do it all again, every day, endlessly, because you're a pony farmer, and that is your life. Paradise on Earth! Right? Right!

Presumably, if the *Pony Farm* was also located in France, German language wisdom dictates it would at least double the enjoyment, because then you could say you *live life like God on a pony farm in France.*

Nice is the little brother of shit
(Nett ist der kleine Bruder von Scheiße)

I really appreciate how German culture doesn't force false niceties upon everyone all the time. One does not just smile because one has entered a shop. One does not ask how someone is, unless someone cares how someone is. The easiest way to learn what is genuine, after all, is to first identify what is false. German culture allows for this. When I first started dating my German girlfriend, I made the mistake of asking questions that I might not like the answer to. Such as »Did you enjoy the dinner I prepared? What do you think of my brother? Do I look good in this striped shirt? How was the sex?«

With previous English girlfriends, I would have expected an empty but not unpleasant-sounding combination of »wow … it/he/she/they …was/is/are/ …great!/amazing!/brilliant!« While pleasing to the ear, *nice* rarely helps anyone. Criticism encourages self-reflection. Restriction is good for creativity. Opinions solve problems. Often in an attempt to not inconvenience, you actually just end up further inconveniencing.

Recently my girlfriend was talking to me about the upcoming visit of my parents for Christmas and what she could do to contribute. »Shall I cook a meal for them?« she asked.

»If you want,« I said.

»What if they don't like it?«

»It doesn't really matter, they won't say, they'll just say it's great and amazing and the best meal since The Last Supper.«

»What's the point then? If I won't get an honest answer, and I can't fail, the fun's gone from trying.«

My point exactly. Wise Germans, understanding that *nice is the little brother of shit*, tend to just say exactly what they think without any mental filters involved. »The dinner was too salty, your brother really needs to act his age, that shirt accentuates your gut, the sex was too elbowy. Other than that, everything's perfectly *in Ordnung*, I guess.«

Thank you

So, dearly beloved Denglischer, we find ourselves now at the end of this humble little book of language muddling. We hope that our short tour of the German language's most exciting opportunities has entertained you, and we wish you much success in bringing the new international language of Denglisch to the unsuspecting foreign masses!

Since this is where we would traditionally *Auf Wiedersehen*, first a few short mentions of thanks. Firstly and most importantly, we would like to thank Annett and Linn – our Primary Expat Carers – who for the duration of this book have been clumsily combined into the singular role of »German girlfriend«. Thank you both for being such wonderful, entertaining, willing, and ever present case studies of the German condition. Without you, there is no doubt we would be anecdote-less, and probably in prison for ignoring all those scary, official looking letters you always deal with for us.

Also, thanks to all of the anonymous strangers of the internet who've created, shared, and posted various lists of many of the Denglisch phrases we've used in this book. In particular, thanks to the website www.ithinkispider.com, the biggest and best of those lists. A similar thanks must go to Gabi for being the offline version of those lists – a living, giggling encyclopedia of German idioms.

Lastly, thanks to all of the kind and quirky people we've

vor sich gehen? Gäbe es ein landesweites Referendum, bei dem wir alle abstimmen könnten, welches Geschlecht das Wort »*hermaphrodite*« bekommen soll? Das würde nicht funktionieren.

Wir könnten auch eine Fernsehlotterie daraus machen. Eine Lottofee in einem hautengen Kleid würde lächelnd ankündigen, dass das Hauptwort des heutigen Abends »*ventriloquist*« (= Bauchredner) sei und dass der anwesende Notar sich vom ordnungsgemäßen Zustand der je 100 Kugeln mit der Aufschrift »der«, »die« und »das« überzeugt habe. Dann würde die Trommel sich in Bewegung setzen und schließlich eine Kugel mit »das« ausspucken, dem künftigen Artikel des Worts »ventriloquist«.

Natürlich liegt unser Fehler beim Hadern mit den deutschen Geschlechtern darin, dass wir nach einer logischen Verbindung zwischen den benannten Dingen und ihrem grammatischen Geschlecht suchen. Wir wollen eben alles personifizieren. Wir wollen Hauptwörtern wie »Katze« und »Maus« Kleidchen anziehen und sie schminken, oder dem »Hund« eine Hose verpassen. Dabei kann man die Sache nur verstehen, wenn man kapiert, dass das Geschlecht sich nach dem Wort richtet und nicht nach der durch das Wort benannten Sache.

Wenn man das mal begriffen hat, kann man ganz mechanisch lernen, dass Wörter auf -heit, -keit, -schaft und -ung fast immer weiblich sind, während Wörter auf -ling, -ich, -en, und -er männlichen Geschlechts sind. Man kann entspannt und freudig genießen, was für grandiose Missverständnisse die Geschlechter der deutschen Sprache bringen können. Wie bei dem Mann, der losging, ein Pferdchen zu kaufen, und mit einer neuen Frisur heimkam. Oder beim

Mus / Mousse, das nach einer schweren Identitätskrise mit einer Der-die-das-Diagnose in der Psychiatrie gelandet ist. Oder bei dem türkischen Autoverkäufer, der zum Internet-Star wurde und dessen Verkaufszahlen durch die Decke gingen, weil er ein Auto als »der Gerät« statt »das Gerät« angepriesen hatte. Er wurde in eine Fernsehshow eingeladen, nur um seinen kleinen Grammatikfehler mit erotischer Komponente zu wiederholen. Und eine Million Leute sahen sich das auf YouTube an.

Ich glaube inzwischen, dass die deutsche Sprache genauso funktioniert wie das Kartenspiel Mao: Die Deutschen behaupten steif und fest, es gebe Regeln, aber sie weigern sich standhaft, dir diese Regeln mitzuteilen – weil sie sich so darüber amüsieren, wenn du lustige Fehler machst.

Denglisch Wisdom

Who won't listen must feel

Die Deutschen müssen sich nicht für ihre Sprache und deren Eigenheiten rechtfertigen. Sie leben in dem Bewusstsein, dass ihre Sprache der Schlüssel zum weltbesten Schatz uralten Wissens ist. Da kommt nicht jeder rein. Eine Abkürzung zur Erleuchtung gibt's nun mal nicht. Weisheit muss man sich verdienen. Deutschland hat sich seit jeher in tadelloser Weise bewährt auf den Feldern der Philosophie, der Literatur und nicht zuletzt der Poesie. Deutsch, das ist die Sprache von Bach, Nietzsche, Kant, Marx, Goethe und vielen anderen bedeutenden Toten, die viele schlaue Dinge sagten, an denen die Lebenden bis heute rumknabbern.

Entsprechend schwierig war es, für dieses Kapitel eine Auswahl aus diesem Schatz der deutschen Weisheit zu treffen. Ob es nun um das *holy Indian-honour-word* (heiliges Indianerehrenwort) geht, *that went in the trousers* (das ging in die Hose), *he who fries someone else's sausage has a sausage-frying-device* (Wer andern eine Bratwurst brät, der hat ein Bratwurst-Bratgerät), *sometimes even blind chickens can also find corn* (selbst ein blindes Huhn findet manchmal ein Korn), *well-known like a colorful dog* (bekannt wie ein bunter Hund), oder darum *to add your mustard everywhere* (überall seinen Senf dazugeben). Am Ende haben wir uns schließlich schweren Herzens für die folgenden sechs Fundstücke entschieden.

Remember, you're going to die
(Bedenke, dass du sterben musst)

Berufsjugendliche haben jüngst den englischen Satz »*you only live once*« zum kürzeren und peppigeren Akronym *YOLO* verballhornt. Das rufen sie vermutlich als permanente Rechtfertigungsformel, während sie völlig idiotische Dinge tun, die ihre Gesundheit oder zumindest die ihrer Genitalien gefährden. Die Formel YOLO ist zum Brandbeschleuniger kompletter Dämlichkeit geworden. Für Leute, die in Fässer steigen und einen steilen Hang runterrollen. Für das besoffene Herumbalancieren auf Balkonbrüstungen und Dächern. Für *chest-bumpings* mit einem Schaufenster.

Die durch und durch spaßbefreite, etwas altmodische deutsche Formulierung »*remember, you're going to die*« gibt keinerlei Raum für solche Idiotien. Sie dient dazu, uns zu erden und mit Demut statt mit Dämlichkeit zu erfüllen. Weil sie nicht so sehr die Lebensfreude betont, sondern die Gewissheit des Todes. Voll der Stimmungskiller. Die Redewendung sagt: »Du wirst sterben, kleiner Timmy, und zwar schon sehr bald, genauer gesagt, in wenigen Sekunden, wenn du nicht umgehend von diesem Dach runterkommst. Wodka-Red-Bull hin oder her: Du kannst nicht fliegen. Und das da sind auch keine Flügel, sondern die Vorhänge aus dem Wohnzimmer, du besoffener Trottel.«

Is it art – or can I chuck it?
(Ist das Kunst – oder kann das weg?)

In London gibt es ein Museum namens *The Tate Modern*. Es ist sehr groß und enthält Kunst. Und Müll. Manchmal sieht der Müll aus wie Kunst. Manchmal ist es umgekehrt. Und manchmal i s t der Müll Kunst. Oder umgekehrt. Oder die Kunst besteht aus Müll. Oder umgekehrt. Alles sehr verwirrend. Und sehr modern.

Gleich rechts, wenn man reinkommt, kann man beispielsweise ein altes, ungemachtes Bett bestaunen, das möglicherweise einen renommierten Kunstpreis gewonnen hat und eine sechsstellige Summe wert ist. Stünde es fünf Meter weiter vorne, auf dem Bürgersteig vor dem Gebäude, würde es umgehend von vierschrötigen Männern in orangenen Westen auf Kosten des Steuerzahlers abtransportiert.

Der wunderbare Denglisch-Ausdruck »*Is it art – or can I chuck it?*« lässt jedem blasierten Kunstkenner erst mal die Luft ab und erinnert jeden Künstler daran, dass er Kunst, die aus irgendeinem Grund mit Müll verwechselt werden könnte, stets mit einer guten Begründung dafür versehen sollte, warum sie zusammen mit eindrucksvollen Gemälden und Skulpturen in einem Museum stehen muss, statt direkt davor auf der Straße als Katzenklo dient.

Live like God in France
(Leben wie Gott in Frankreich)

Dass die Deutschen Frankreich lieben, liegt auf der Hand. Die Anziehungskraft, die insbesondere Paris auf die »boches«

ausübt, ist historisch vielfach belegt. Möglicherweise gibt diese Formulierung einen Hinweis auf die Gründe dieser Zuneigung. Wie alle Comedy-Autoren bin ich allerdings sehr skeptisch gegenüber nationalen Stereotypen. Hüstel. Wenn ich diese Skepsis aber mal hinten anstellen würde, dann würde ich der deutschen Überzeugung zustimmen, dass das höchste Ziel eines jeden Menschen nur darin bestehen kann, allmächtig und allwissend zu sein und sich dabei im Land des Croissants aufzuhalten. Dann könnte man zur Mittagszeit frühstücken und dabei ein Päckchen Gauloises rauchen, eine Flasche Rotwein trinken, sich einen Schnurrbart wachsen lassen, die Welt erschaffen, eine existentialistische Diskussion über die Sinnlosigkeit dieser Schöpfung anzetteln, stundenlang Sex haben und den Arbeitstag gegen drei Uhr nachmittags beenden. Was könnte besser sein als das? *Vive la D'anglais!*

Everything has an ending only the sausage has two
(Alles hat ein Ende, nur die Wurst hat zwei)

Auch der lernwilligste Ausländer wird Schwierigkeiten haben, die Gültigkeit dieser Weisheit anzuerkennen – zum einen vielleicht wegen seiner Sturheit, aber vor allem wohl weil es einfach Blödsinn ist. Wenn du diesen Satz von dir gibst, kriegst du höchstwahrscheinlich so eine Antwort: »Also, jetzt mal ehrlich: Nach dieser Logik hat doch alles, was länglich ist, zwei Enden – und nicht nur die Wurst. Was ist mit Zahnpasta? Vorhangstangen? Bananen? Und diese kleinen Hunde – wie heißen die noch mal? Ach ja, *Dachshunde*.«

Wenn das geschieht, solltest du mit dramatischer Geste hinausstürmen und dich nur noch mal umdrehen, um auszurufen: »Ihr wollt es einfach nicht kapieren, was?«, oder aber: »Ja, ja, der *Dachshund* – auch so ein Wort, das die deutsche Sprache dem Englischen geschenkt hat, um ihm ein wenig auf die Beine zu helfen. Keiner von euch ahnt, dass in Deutschland niemand das Wort *Dachshund* benutzt, wenn er einen Dackel meint. Ha!«

Life is not a pony farm
(Das Leben ist kein Ponyhof)

Die Deutschen sind nicht empfänglich für billige, kindische Vorstellungen eines Utopia. Sie sind Realisten und wissen, dass in diesem rätselhaften Dasein die größte Annäherung an das wahre und vollendete Glück ein Job auf einem Ponyhof wäre. Stell dir vor: Du dürftest jeden Tag früh aufstehen, das Futter für all die vielen Ponys vorbereiten, sie alle füttern, sie alle raus auf die Weide bringen, sie alle im Kreis führen, sie alle wieder füttern, sie alle striegeln, eine Schaufel nehmen und die stinkende Kacke all der vielen Ponys aus den Ställen und von deinen Beinen kratzen, sie wieder füttern, sie wieder striegeln, wieder Kacke wegmachen, füttern, im Kreis führen – und abends schmeißt du dann all deine Klamotten in die Waschmaschine, versuchst, den Ponykackegeruch von dir selbst abzuwaschen, gehst ins Bett und fängst am nächsten Morgen wieder von vorne an. All die vielen Ponys. Jeden Tag. In alle Ewigkeit. Denn du hast einen Ponyhof. Das ist dein Leben. Es ist das Paradies auf Erden, oder? Jawoll!

Läge die *Pony Farm* in Frankreich, wäre das größte deutsche Glücksversprechen ganz sicher: *Life is living like a God in a pony farm in France.*

Nice is the little brother of shit
(Nett ist der kleine Bruder von Scheiße)

Die Deutschen haben keinerlei Neigung zu falschen Nettigkeiten. Ich finde das gut. Wieso sollte man lächeln, nur weil ein Kunde den Laden betritt? Wieso sollte man fragen, wie es jemandem geht, wenn er einem scheißegal ist? Was richtig ist, kann man schließlich nur lernen, wenn einem gesagt wird, was falsch ist. Als ich meine Freundin kennenlernte, beging ich anfangs den Fehler, Fragen zu stellen, auf die ich keine ehrliche Antwort hören wollte. Wie zum Beispiel »Hat dir mein Essen geschmeckt?«, »Was hältst du von meinem Bruder?«, »Wie steht mir dieses geringelte T-Shirt?«, »Wie war ich?« Meine englischen Exfreundinnen hätten darauf mit einem vielleicht etwas hohl, aber durchaus angenehm klingenden *»wow… it/he/she/they …was/is/are …great!/amazing!/ brilliant!«* geantwortet. Das ist zwar schön, nützt aber niemandem. Nur Kritik regt das Nachdenken über sich selbst an. Erst die Zurückweisung spornt die Kreativität an. Klare Meinungen helfen beim Lösen von Problemen. Der Versuch, einen Affront zu vermeiden, erzeugt oft erst den eigentlichen Affront.

Kürzlich plante meine Freundin unseren Weihnachtsbesuch bei meinen Eltern – und überlegte, was sie zum Fest beitragen könne. »Soll ich etwas kochen?«, fragte sie mich.

»Wenn du Lust hast«, sagte ich.

»Und was ist, wenn es ihnen nicht schmeckt?«

»Das spielt doch keine Rolle. Sie werden sagen, dass es köstlich und super und das beste Essen seit dem Letzten Abendmahl war.«

»Und was hab ich dann davon? Wenn ich keine ehrliche Antwort erwarten und sowieso nichts falsch machen kann, macht es keinen Spaß, es überhaupt zu versuchen.«

So sind sie, die Deutschen. Klug genug, um zu wissen, dass *nice is the little brother of shit*. Sie sagen immer genau das, was sie denken – ohne falsche Rücksicht auf Empfindlichkeiten. »Dein Essen war versalzen, dein Bruder sollte sich endlich mal seinem Alter entsprechend benehmen, das geringelte T-Shirt betont deine Wampe und der Sex war etwas schmerzhaft, dank deines Ellbogeneinsatzes. Aber abgesehen davon ist eigentlich alles in Ordnung, würde ich sagen.«

Dank

So, liebe Denglisch-Schüler, wir sind nun am Ende unseres kleinen Wörterbuchs der Sprachverwurschtelung. Wir hoffen, dass diese Reise zu den aufregendsten Möglichkeiten der deutschen Sprache euch Spaß gemacht hat, und wir wünschen euch viel Erfolg beim Versuch, die Millionen und Abermillionen nichtsahnenden Ausländer mit der neuen Weltsprache Denglisch vertraut zu machen.

An dieser Stelle müsste traditionell *Auf Wiedersehen* stehen. Vorher möchten wir aber einigen Menschen danken. Zuerst und vor allem Annett und Linn, unseren weltbesten Integrationshelfern, die wir für dieses Buch recht dreist zu »meine deutsche Freundin« zusammengerührt haben. Danke euch beiden dafür, dass ihr uns so wunderbar, unterhaltsam, geduldig und unermüdlich gezeigt habt, wie es ist, deutsch zu sein. Ohne euch wäre dieses Buch gänzlich frei von Anekdoten – und wir säßen vermutlich im Gefängnis, weil wir die ganzen offiziellen Behördenschreiben, Rechnungen und Mahnungen ignoriert hätten, um die ihr euch für uns gekümmert habt.

Ein weiterer Dank geht an all die Unbekannten da draußen im Internet, die Listen mit Denglisch-Wendungen erstellt, geteilt und geposted haben, die in dieses Buch eingeflossen sind. Speziell bedanken wir uns bei allen Mitwirkenden der Website www.ithinkispider.com, der größten und besten dieser Listen. Ebenfalls ein spezieller Dank geht an Gabi, die

Offline-Version dieser Internet-Listen – ein lebendiges, immer kicherndes Lexikon deutscher Redewendungen.

Zuletzt wollen wir uns bei all den freundlichen und aufgeweckten Menschen bedanken, die wir in unserer Zeit in Deutschland kennenlernen durften. Kein Zweifel: Nur eure Wärme und Großzügigkeit haben dafür gesorgt, dass wir uns hier wirklich zu Hause fühlen, dass wir gerne hierbleiben und dass wir uns weiter für eure Kultur interessieren. Vielen Dank!

With friendly greetings,
Ädäm Fletscher and Päul Häwkins

FOX DEVIL WILD'S

Denglisch Restaurant

*Looking over the edge
of our plates since 1952*

MENU